WORK
the
SYSTEM

The Simple Mechanics of
Making More and Working Less

SAM CARPENTER

GREENLEAF
BOOK GROUP PRESS
Hillsboro, OR
Member of Washington County
COOPERATIVE LIBRARY SERVICES

Published by Greenleaf Book Group Press
Austin, TX
www.greenleafbookgroup.com

Distributed by Greenleaf Book Group LLC

For ordering information or special discounts for bulk purchases, please contact Greenleaf Book Group LLC at PO Box 91869, Austin, TX 78709, (512) 891-6100.

Design and composition by Greenleaf Book Group LLC
Cover design by Greenleaf Book Group LLC

Publisher's Cataloging-In-Publication Data
(Prepared by The Donohue Group, Inc.)

Carpenter, Sam.
  Work the system : the simple mechanics of making more and working less / Sam Carpenter. -- 2nd ed.

    p. ; cm.

    Previous ed. published: Bend, Ore. : North Sister Publishing, 2008.
    Includes bibliographical references and index.
    ISBN: 978-1-929774-87-6   4124 0176 4/09

1. Organizational effectiveness. 2. Organizational change--Management. 3. Success in business. I. Title.

HD58.9 .C377 2009
658.4/02   2008943859

ISBN: 978-1-929774-87-6

 Part of the Tree Neutral™ program, which offsets the number of trees consumed in the production and printing of this book by taking proactive steps, such as planting trees in direct proportion to the number of trees used: www.treeneutral.com

First edition published 2008
North Sister Publishing Inc., Bend, Oregon

Printed in the United States of America on acid-free paper

09 10 11 12 13 14   10 9 8 7 6 5 4 3 2 1

Second Edition

To Linda, of course

One should choose the simplest explanation,
the one requiring the fewest assumptions and principles.

—WILLIAM OF OCKHAM, FOURTEENTH-CENTURY ENGLISH PHILOSOPHER

Contents

Preface
It's Just Mechanics

I work the system, but not just one. I work all the systems in my control—professional, financial, social, biological, and mechanical. You have your own systems. Do you see them? Do you control them? It doesn't matter whether you are a CEO, an employee, a stay-at-home mom or dad, a retiree, or a student. Your life is composed of systems that are yours to control—or not control.

In the slang sense of the term, someone who "works the system" uses a bureaucratic loophole as an excuse to break rules in order to secure personal gain. But winning the life game means following the rules, for if we don't, any win is a ruse. Be assured that you will find nothing deceitful or unsavory in these pages. Nor does the *Work the System* methodology have anything to do with esoteric theory, politics, or religion. It is about common sense and simple mechanics. I call it a workingman's philosophy.

Life is serious business, and whether you know it or not—or whether you like it or not—your personal systems are the threads of the fabric of your life. Together, your personal systems add up to you. And if you are like most people, you negotiate your days without seeing your systems as the singular entities they are, some working well and some not so well.

In the complexity that is your life, what if you could distinctly see each of these systems? What if you could reach in and pluck a not-so-perfect system out of that complexity, make it perfect, and then reinsert it? What if you could perform this process with every system that composes your life? What if you could reengineer your life piece by piece to make it exactly what you want it to be without having to count on luck, providence, blind faith, or someone else's largesse?

The foundational thrust of *Work the System* is not to educate you in the "ten steps to peace and prosperity," or to warn you of the "five most common mistakes in seeking happiness." The method digs deeper than that. *Work the System* will cause a modification in the way you see your world. And when this quiet yet profound mechanical shift in your perception of life occurs (you will remember the exact moment you "get it"), the simple methodology will make irrefutable sense and you will never be the same.

The book also provides a framework—yes, a compendium of dos and don'ts—through which you can channel this new perspective to get what you want out of your life.

TWO VIEWPOINTS

In a broad sense, there are two psychological approaches to finding a way to lead a full, positive life. The first holds that the events of the past, and the mind-set we form as a result of them, determine today's happiness. In this view, we are victims of unpleasant circumstance and have a chance at peace only if we face and then disarm the psychic monsters planted in our minds long ago. That's the Freudian stance.

The second approach maintains that the thoughts we feed ourselves today are what matter most, and the events of the past are just that—in the past—and gone forever unless we insist on giving them new life by swirling them back into the present moment.

I see the cognitive approach as more practical than the Freudian, because it frees an individual to seize control of the immediate thought process rather than wallowing in negativity from years gone by. I believe that what we do today will determine our tomorrow, and blaming the past, or the world, or someone else is a debilitating way to travel through this precious one-time event called life.

Without question, blue-blooded, old-school psychologists who see endless dour complexity in the human condition will deride the simplicity of the *Work the System* message. Things are more complicated than that, they'll say. I thank them in advance for their oblique compliment. This is an elementary, dispassionate, drop-the-load dispatch that describes lives as they really are: cause-and-effect mechanisms that can be logical, predictable, and satisfying. No PhD necessary.

So take the title of this book at exact literal face value, understanding you will be working *your* systems. In these pages, I challenge you to improve and manage them, to dissect and refine them one by one until each is perfect. (I call this process "system improvement.") You will create new systems, too, while discarding the ones holding you back, the ones that have been invisibly sabotaging your best efforts. Manage the systems of your life and move toward inner serenity, prosperity, and the best for those around you.

LEADER AND HIGH EARNER

Not too long ago I participated in Cycle Oregon, a weeklong bicycle tour. Seventeen hundred riders pedaled an average of seventy-five miles each day through remote eastern Oregon. At night we camped in ad hoc tent cities planted at various locations along the route: rural high school football fields, small town parks, or wheat fields. Seldom did we have cellular telephone coverage. That was just fine as we, en masse, divorced ourselves from the damn things for this seven-day break from the regular world.

At dusk on the last night of the tour, as my friend Steve and I were casually walking through the surrounding sea of tents, we encountered a group of guys in their thirties sitting around drinking beer, being boisterous. We overheard them laughing, waging bets about how many voice mail messages one of their group members would have the next day when he was back within cell phone range and able to check his messages. Clearly, back in the real world these guys worked together in an office. One predicted the total messages would be 250, another, 150. The young man on the receiving end of the jest was robust, clean-cut, and confident. He smiled at the fawning. It was obvious this man was important in his work. He was well respected, a leader, and most probably a high earner—a success. People depended on him.

For twenty-four years I have been general manager and CEO of a small business. Centratel is profitable, has twenty-five employees, and has a solid, loyal client base. The part I play is important; in my world, I'm also a leader and high earner. Many depend on me, too.

When I checked my voice mail the next day as I began the long drive home, there was just one message. Andi, my COO, had left a general and benign update because she knew I would be interested in getting caught up on things when I was able to pick up my messages again. She reported that all was well in the office and she hoped I had had a fun week away from things. "Drive home safely," she said. That was it. She didn't need to address the obvious: During the week, without a hitch and without an ounce of input from me, the business had functioned perfectly while it continued to churn out thousands of dollars in profits. It didn't matter that I was absent.

Who knows what that voice mail–inundated young man does for a living, but I tell you this: He is mismanaging things if his world can't proceed for a single week without his direct influence; if the myriad systems in which he is involved all come to a halt when he is not available. Yes, all those voice mail messages attest to his status and importance, but in the bigger picture, he is a slave to his job. And the people who depend on him are slaves to his presence. They wait for his next call and can't move ahead until he provides input. In his absence, because he fails to set up business systems that keep producing while he is gone, things come to a standstill in the same way water accumulates behind a dam.

He was about thirty years of age; I'm fifty-nine. People and circumstances change with time. Not too long ago, my life was just like his.

HOOKED UP

Here's another, more general observation: In the past thirty years, the lure of instant gratification has gripped a large chunk of our population. For the hooked-up masses—those who are seriously addicted to iPods and Blackberries and the immediacy/pervasiveness of the entertainment industry—it's a stretch to go backward to consider the root of things. The gratification of the moment is a distraction from thoughtful contemplation of the reasons why events happen as they do. Today, unlike thirty years ago, a good "now" is available by just turning off and plugging in. For too many of us, slowing down to examine things is not entertaining, and that's too bad because it is mandatory that we understand the machinery of our lives if we are to modify that machinery to produce the results we want.

Yes, *Work the System* is a throwback of sorts, back to an age when there was thoughtful preparation with no expectation of immediate payback. But having said that, know that an investment in the *Work the System* strategy will show quick tangible benefits. Maybe not tomorrow, but certainly within a few weeks.

CLOSED-SYSTEM LABORATORY

Centratel is a high-tech telephone answering service. For fifteen years it foundered, my personal life a reflection of its chaos. However, over the last few years, as I applied the protocols that are described here, my work-week became a fraction of what it was as my income increased twentyfold. Moreover, my life away from work is smooth and easy now, with plenty of extra time to do the things I have always wanted to do. In the morning I awake serene, looking forward to yet another day of quiet, steady improvement on all fronts. In the course of a week, I spend far more time reading, writing, going to the movies, climbing mountains, and riding bicycles than working. My life is in control. It's what I want it to be.

The nature of the telephone-answering service business, with its multitude of interacting systems, both human and otherwise, made Centratel the perfect closed-system laboratory for developing the *Work the System* methodology. It is logical and convenient to use my business as the explanatory platform for these chaos-to-order processes. And things can get too dry and theoretical without real-life examples, so describing the method within the framework of Centratel adds some life to the party.

The strategies described here are not just for the small business owner; they are also for those who work in a management capacity for a business owned by someone else. There are lessons for those born with a silver spoon and for the self-made wealthy, too. We will be dealing with reality, and reality works in the same way for everyone, everywhere, all the time, so when I offer a personal business illustration, read between the lines and find your own application—professional or personal.

And when I refer to my business and use the word "manager," understand that the label also applies to personal life. We are the managers of our lives, and the foundational protocols described here are universal.

The principles of the *Work the System* method are simple, but it is not enough to memorize or understand them. They must be internalized, deep down. There is a difference between learning something new and undergoing a visceral epiphany. On a gut level, "getting it" is key. For this reason, in part one some repetition will occur as I approach the concepts from different angles. Trust that the epiphany will come soon.

A qualifier: I don't adhere to the *Work the System* principles and guidelines every minute. I fall down on the job now and then. Nonetheless, because I have structured my life around the methodology, the details of the day continue to take care of themselves despite any temporary distraction or physical/mental slump. My hyperefficient systems keep things moving forward no matter what.

The same will hold for you too, should you buy into the method and choose to take firm control of your life.

Acknowledgments

Thank you to Sam Kirkaldie, my partner, for your calm strength; Andi Freeman, for your faith in me and our systems—you really "get it" as you watch my back; Hollee Wilson, for also "getting it" and being on top of every situation, never, ever letting me down; Pattie Casner, for your superb work and enduring the hard times; Lannie Dell, our longest-term employee, for sticking it out through eighteen years; Sandra Packard, our seventeen-year veteran, for your insistence on perfection and for weathering those storms; Linda Morgan, for your dependability and calm demeanor; Carla Hoekstra, for always being there to do what must be done; Denise Jones, for your nonstop, positive contribution; Dan Blomquist, for being our master of the IT universe—and undisputed gadget champion of the world; Shannon Walker, for your calm, steady let's-get-to-it comportment; and the Centratel staff, for the smile in your voices. You are the cream of the crop and the heart of our success.

Twenty years ago, Lindsay Stevens gave me my first inkling that a business should be managed, not indulged; Reese Shepard insisted there be a plan; Roger Shields, retired banker, smacked me in the head with his air-bat when I needed it most; Robert Killen, of Columbia River Bank, gave me a break when everyone else equivocated; "RC" Roger Christensen, former President of Columbia River Bank, cut me slack when the two of us were at the bottom of our respective career ladders; NYS Ranger School faculty taught me about common sense and hard work; and Lane Powell, my mentor, now deceased, left his mark on my life.

Special thanks to editors Jay Hodges, Linda O'Doughda, and Theresa Reding, and to the rest of the Greenleaf gang. Also to my father,

Tom Carpenter, freelancers Sarah Max and Linda Chestney, for preliminary editing.

Thank you, Natalie Troyer, my assistant/publicist, for your relentless efforts to get the word out, and Anne Pietz, my wonderful mother-in-law, for your nitpicky input.

Thank you, daughter Jennifer, for confirming that a penchant for living on the edge is indeed a genetic trait.

Thanks to Khizar Abassi, for assisting me in helping the back-country people of Azad Jammu Kashmir; Ahsan and Mina Rashid, for showing Linda and me the real Pakistan.

To my brother Steve Carpenter, who can put the abstract in a nutshell and do it with humor (thanks too, for your contribution to the space shuttle illustration); to Jack Cornelius for his "Great Machine" story. And Linda Carpenter, for your incredible patience and invariably on-target suggestions.

To the men and women of our military, thank you for your sacrifice. Your song is not sung enough.

INTRODUCTION

The Simplest Solution

Out of clutter, find simplicity. From discord, find harmony.

—ALBERT EINSTEIN

One should choose the simplest explanation of a phenomenon, the one that requires the fewest leaps of logic. Or one could say, "Keep it simple, stupid!"

My wife, Linda, and I live on the outskirts of a vibrant mountain resort town in the great American Northwest. Our house is not large, but it's open and bright, furnished in a pragmatic, people-actually-live-here way. For each of us, it is everything we have ever wanted in a home.

I sit at the dining room table in front of my laptop. Outside the window, the quiet of the late afternoon is tangible. It's June. The lawn is lush green and is the launching pad for a half dozen huge ponderosa pines towering above the house. The weather is warm—another perfect, cloudless day in Central Oregon. Yesterday was like that and tomorrow will be the same.

It's peaceful. Linda sits at the table next to me, and we chat.

Meanwhile, in town, my telephone answering service business churns away whether we're thinking about it or not, providing more than a good living for us. It wasn't always this way. For fifteen years, my business experience was a chaotic morass of endless work, fire-killing, debt, health problems, and bad relationships.

Over the past few years, my life has moved from tumult to focused calm. Nine years ago, at a single point in time, I experienced an unexpected shift in perception that began the transformation of my existence. Now, truly managing my small business and my life, I am no longer enmeshed in minutiae but am an arm's-length observer of it. The numbers are good: Compared to just a few years ago, my workweek is two hours instead of a hundred, and my earnings in a month far exceed what I used to make in a year. My health is back, too; I'm climbing, cycling, and skiing again.

As for the subjective? It's no stretch to say my life has ten times more peace and freedom. Much of the time, as my day slides by, I feel like an athlete in the zone: powerful, relaxed, and efficient.

Getting to this place wasn't hard to do once I tweaked my mind-set to view each day from a more intimate angle. Since seizing upon this deeper reality, I have been able to channel my efforts to get what I want from life. Did I have to work hard? Yes, for a short while there was some hard work. But in comparison to the nightmare of my previous life, the effort was not much and I was happy to do it, especially as the results began to roll in.

How I did this—and how you can do the same—is the grist of this book.

I direct *Work the System* to those who have the following chronic internal dialogue: "There are things I must do right now, and there is barely the time or money or energy to do them. I will bulldoze my way through these tasks, and as usual, they will be completed just in time—but the results will be of marginal quality, and my body and mind will continue to be stretched to the breaking point. I'm tired and stressed and can't seem to shake free of living on the edge, and I worry about my frame of mind and my health. There is too much chaos around me, too little control, and never enough money—things are far from what they should be . . ."

If you own or manage a small business, have a job, or are a student, there's a good chance the above dialogue caught your attention. In our Western world, I'm-just-barely-hanging-on self-talk is endemic to every class of people and every age group.

I'm a low-key guy. Not a lot of flash, no frills, and no advanced college degree. I've run the standard gauntlet of ups and downs, successes and failures, and like a lot of folks, I've worked hard all my life. It's clear to me that pragmatism increases with age, we live by trial and error, and lessons can be learned from being banged around. Further, I'm not afraid to face cold reality, and I exhibit a knee-jerk suspicion of unsupportable theory. I have a single, limited time-span life, and I treasure this life gift. My life is managed now, planned and maintained. Work or play, it gets my full attention.

No, of course I haven't got the world neatly tied up in a bag (who does?), but I have found a way to take control, to make the days of my life orderly and calm. I wake up almost every day alert, strong, and happy.

COMPLEX JUMBLE?

What about you? How do you describe your typical day? Is it an amorphous, complex jumble of happenings, or is it a relaxed and ordered sequence of events? Is it chaotic, or is it under control? Do you have enough money? Do you spend enough time with friends and family? Through the day—and through your life—are you in an endless race around a circular track, or are you climbing slowly and steadily toward a mountaintop? Are you getting what you want? If not, could it be a personal management problem?

Don't confuse these questions with right, wrong, good, or bad, and don't inject some abstract theoretical, political, or religious aspect into your answers. Keep this mechanical and—equally important—keep it simple. And take heart. If you tend toward defining your life as a complex jumble of events, rest assured that you already have 100 percent of the resources you'll need to eliminate this too-common story line. You'll just have to assemble the pieces of your day in a different way.

The *Work the System* method is almost silly in its simplicity but nothing less than profound in its capacity to transform. That's why I chose the words of William of Ockham for the epigraph of my book: the simplest solution *is* invariably the most correct solution. Here, as I begin to discuss recognizable events and scenarios, habits, goals, successes, failures, and plain old common sense, you will relate to the *Work the System* methodology because it is believable. It is about simple mechanical improvements that will combine to transform your existence.

Yet what I describe in these pages is not apparent to the casual observer.

This book is not about feel-good, pie-in-the-sky promises. Here there are no new-think premises nor is there pseudo-intellectual blathering. You will not be asked to write down tedious lists, memorize odd platitudes, repeat affirmations, make daily journal entries, publicize your newfound direction to your friends and family, or worst of all, wait to see if yet another mysterious theory will make things better. This isn't a matter of blind faith.

But if you think sheer energy, clever thinking, and unbounded enthusiasm are enough to secure the freedom and income you want, think a bit further. Certain structures—certain systems—must be in place before these important attributes can take you where you want to go. Freedom and wealth occur *after* the mechanics are in place.

So is there something you must do, some work that you must perform? Yes, with the *Work the System* method, you will produce some written documentation. And, if you manage people, you will teach them your new vision. But you're working and supervising anyway, right? The *Work the System* method asks you to channel these same allotments of time and energy toward incremental step-by-step building efforts that lead to freedom, prosperity, and peace.

And think again about racing around an endless circle versus a steady upward climb toward a goal. Effort is required either way, but know it is the climbing you want. Instead of expending precious time and energy on getting-nowhere, churning tedium (which is the hardest and most frustrating work of all), you will expend that same time and energy in a step-by-step steady climb that will provide a geometric return on investment.

The *Work the System* method deals with a mechanical fact that most people overlook, a can't-see-the-forest-for-the-trees myopia. The system-based protocols discussed here are quietly used in large, successful businesses and organizations everywhere, but they are not often present in small businesses. And although the principles of the method are scattered among scores of business, religious, and pop-psychology writings, here they are grouped together in an everyman's methodology that is rooted in one fundamental truth: A life's mechanical functioning is a result of the systems that compose it.

And the simple crux of the *Work the System* method? It's this: If it is true that "a life's mechanical functioning is a result of the systems that compose it," then getting what you want in life does not lie in manipulating outcomes; doing that is a distraction. Rather, getting what you want lies in delving deeper, in focusing on "working the systems" that *create* the results. Hence, the title of this book: *Work the System*. The first task—the "getting it" part—is to discover and then constantly see these separate systems in each moment of the day. Once that happens, "working" them is simple, and the results will take care of themselves.

CONSCIOUSLY PAYING ATTENTION

All of us have recurring personal systems we employ to good advantage. We have many systems "down pat," systems that are efficient and quick because we have honed the details to perfection. We have perfected driving a car, fixing breakfast, and attending to a repeated minor challenge at work. Why are we expert in these small processes? Because they are simple, yes, but mostly because at some point we consciously paid close attention to those processes; we analyzed and adjusted them so we could do them with little effort, almost without thinking. But for many people, there is no deliberate effort to isolate and study the sequential workings of more complex wide-angle processes like careers and relationships. Some of us just churn along without direction, wasting time and energy revisiting the same problems over and over again.

In order to tackle the more involved challenges of our lives—the challenges that have stymied us because of their complexities—the *Work the System* methodology expands the perceptive, investigative, and analytical skills we already possess. There is nothing new here, just a new approach.

YOUR MENTAL POSTURE

The *Work the System* mind-set is different from the mental posture most people carry around with them from day to day. Instead of seeing yourself as an internal component of circumstances, enmeshed within the day's swirling events, your *Work the System* vantage point is outside and slightly elevated from those events. The day's happenings are visible as separate and individual elements, arranged in logical sequences. You are an observer looking down on things, examining the comings and goings of the day as if they are tangible, physical objects. Things are simple and understandable. Wherever you look, the machinations of the world make sense: Step-by-step, one thing leads to another as the systems around you continuously execute.

You constantly work on those systems. You make them better, one by one. Over time, complexity and confusion decrease to be replaced by order, calm, and rock-solid self-confidence. There is little fire-killing and little confusion, and as you continue to peer down at your handiwork, watching your solid progress toward your goal of freedom, you feel an intense self-respect and you are proud of what you've accomplished.

I COME TO YOU AS A PROJECT ENGINEER

With blue-collar roots, I have a personal background that is a mixed bag: land surveyor, heavy-equipment operator, factory worker, door-to-door salesman, technical consultant, hamburger flipper, house painter, department store sales clerk, construction superintendent, project engineer, ditch digger, sales professional, builder, janitor, journalist, public speaker, book publisher, retail store owner, lab technician, logger, mill worker, stock and commodities investor, writer, photojournalist, telecommunications entrepreneur, real estate salesman, kitchen worker, handyman, corporate CEO, and business owner. I founded and continue to oversee a nonprofit organization that assists earthquake victims in northeast Pakistan and Azad Jammu and Kashmir (see kashmirfamily.org). Through my business, Centratel (centratel.com), my special expertise is in the practical methodology of telecommunications: taking information, processing it, and then passing it on.

Now my overall life role is as a project engineer: that is, someone who accepts a problem, designs a mechanical solution, and then makes that solution work in the real world. I'm a project engineer in every aspect of my life including the personal roles of father, son, brother, husband, and friend.

Metaphorically, here's my day: After a solid night's sleep, I bounce out of bed, shower, eat a big breakfast, and plow into things full bore, plunging deep into the new day. Today I am working with my crew to build something tangible out of the design I created on the drafting table just yesterday. I'm on the job in clean jeans, work boots, and a decent shirt. My persona is relaxed, with a slight smile on my face just under the surface of my focused comportment.

Again, metaphorically, I pull the levers and push the buttons of the unfolding day. My crew and I are lighthearted, relaxed, powerful, and efficient—and we're fast. Work feels good and time flies as we cut a wide swath, making positive things happen, translating yesterday's paper design into the reality of the physical world today. We're creating something worthwhile. We're permanently improving things.

A NON-HOLISTIC APPROACH

Is there a "holistic" or "global" side of you that is balking at separating things out and then examining them individually? You may say everything is connected and we're all one, and we must stop seeing ourselves as separate from the world around us. You may think our lives have unfathomable complexity, way beyond human comprehension. That's fine for the big picture. I tend to think that way myself when I am relaxed and daydreaming. But for now, here in the material world where you must navigate moment to moment, put all that aside and go with the case for separation and simple mechanics.

Understand that fixing an entire scattered conglomeration of a life in one fell swoop is impossible. It can't be done "holistically," despite the rightness that term suggests. Fixing anything of complexity requires proceeding one step at a time, one component at a time—a decidedly non-holistic approach.

I don't care for the term "holistic solution." Instead, I like the term "holistic result," which suggests that each component system within the organism is functioning at peak capacity, resulting in an organism that is superb in fulfilling its purpose.

So it's okay to take things apart to examine them, to get things straightened out piece by piece. You can view things holistically later, when you're not working on the details. There will be plenty of time for that.

CHANGES IN YOUR LIFE

Because this isn't a mystery novel, and because preparation is at the heart of the *Work the System* method, here's a two-part summary of how it will affect you, and what it asks.

First, here are four general points about how the *Work the System* process will impact you personally.

1. **You will undergo an elementary yet fundamental shift in perspective.** This will come to you as a stark awakening in a moment of time rather than over a long, drawn-out learning experience. After it happens, moment-to-moment throughout your day, you will dispassionately observe the human and mechanical systems that comprise your world. These systems will stand apart from each other, starkly visible and sharply defined.

2. **There will be no turning back.** You can't go back! So point two is a warning of sorts. Because of the obvious truth of it, this new "systems perspective" is something you won't be able to shake.

3. **You will not be swallowing unsupportable theories of reality.** This is because there is nothing new here. It's just a matter of tweaking your perception of life's mechanical workings. Plenty enough reality exists without having to delve into esoteric, unsupportable, feel-good theory. Deep down you will know the truth of the *Work the System* method because it makes logical sense and it feels correct. Be assured that you won't sound flighty when explaining your new point of view to those around you. You're not going to lose your friends and family because you are not going to ask them for anything. You have nothing to sell. Instead, should they ask, you will explain what *Work the System* is about, and they will be intrigued with what you have to say.

4. **There is some heavy lifting.** Yes, you will undergo an exciting change of perspective, but that is not enough. At the beginning of the process there is some heavy lifting as you create documentation. That's okay. It's a superb investment because the end product will be freedom, a relaxed persona, and plenty of money. It will

probably be the best investment of time and effort you will ever make.

Here's the second part of this nutshell summary, the three steps of the *Work the System* method.

1. **Documentation:** Creating written goals, principles, and processes that are guidelines for action and decision making. This is the one-time heavy lifting. It won't take long.

2. **Separation, dissection, and repair of systems:** The satisfying process of exposing, analyzing, and then perfecting personal, work, and relationship systems. This effort includes creating new systems from scratch as well as eliminating those that are unnecessary or are holding you back.

3. **Ongoing maintenance of systems:** Greasing the wheels. This is easy because the positive tangible results of the *Work the System* method are motivating. Because it's obvious the systems you create and maintain are doing more and more of your regular daily work, you will continue to make adjustments in order to keep them working at peak efficiency.

TWO ITEMS OF NOTE

First, at the end of most chapters I've placed real-life examples to illustrate various aspects of the *Work the System* method. Some relate to the previous chapter, some don't.

The examples will remind you that the essence of the method is to view your life from a new perspective. This new vantage point is "outside and slightly elevated." Only from an exterior vantage point can systems be examined and adjusted. From this vantage point you can then "reach down" to manipulate those mechanics to produce the results you want.

Second, it's important that we speak the same language. Because all of the following terms appear in part one, I advise you to review them carefully now, particularly because I define these words as they apply to the *Work the System* method.

"99.9 percent of everything works fine": It's the truth! There is a penchant for efficiency in the world; systems want to work perfectly, and most of them do.

Business: One does not have to show up in order to earn money.

Error of omission: A less-than-perfect situation that occurs because someone didn't do something. It is the cause of the majority of problems in the world and in personal lives.

General operating principles: The second of the three primary *Work the System* documents; a two- to four-page collection of "Guidelines for Decision Making" that is congruent with the strategic objective. Essential for the work environment and, in a simplified and shorter format, for one's personal life. (See chapter 10.)

Job or profession: One has to show up in order to earn money.

Linear: For our purposes, this is how most systems execute themselves, in a 1-2-3 stepped progression. Yes, there are always minor external and internal variables that prompt physicists to construe that systems are, strictly speaking, nonlinear. But here in the real world, we are streamlining things so events can be understood and manipulated. A linear system is not chaotic; within its context it is logical, reliable, simple to understand, and simple to improve.

Off-the-street people: These are the people who will "do the work" as viewed by business owners or managers. Depending on the situation, off-the-street workers can be novices or professionals. But because of your thorough documentation and systems strategies, they don't need to be mind readers or fortune-tellers, and they don't necessarily need specific experience in a given field in order to perform superbly.

Outside and slightly elevated: The essential perspective of the *Work the System* methodology is external and above. The view downward also encompasses the viewer. Objectively, we see ourselves below, as separate and distinct, which is the opposite of the common vantage point in which the viewer is integral to the workings of his or her day.

Perfect: In the *Work the System* world, 98 percent accuracy is "perfect" because trying to achieve that additional 2 percent demands too much additional energy. It's the law of diminishing returns in action, and it's a catch-22: The enormous energy required for this tiny increment of improvement is in itself imperfection because that energy could have been put to much better use elsewhere.

Primary system, or system of systems: Composed of subsystems; a whole, encapsulated entity with an ultimate purpose; an organism unto itself, such as a personal life, business, job, car, or relationship.

Project engineer: The role of a business owner or manager who adopts an outside, system-improvement/system-management posture rather than an inside, doing-the-work role. For a personal life, it's real-time positioning in which one's systems are contemplated, analyzed, and then controlled.

Recurring: A process that happens over and over again.

Strategic objective: The first of three primary *Work the System* documents. It's a single page that defines overall goals, describes methodology, and prescribes action; it will serve as an individual's thought-out and carefully constructed "guidebook" to give direction for making major and minor decisions. It is an essential instrument for a business and for a personal life. (See chapter 10.)

System improvement: The heart of the method. A search-and-repair process that involves tooling a system into perfection and then, in one's workplace, documenting that system so its perfect functioning will recur. It is the day-to-day mind-set of a manager, the prime responsibility of an organizational leader. In one's personal life, it's an embedded inclination to seek out and identify personal systems, then to hone each to perfection.

System management: A focus on maximizing the efficiencies of systems in order to prevent recurring problems, to increase production, and to garner more personal time. It tackles a problem by considering the root cause of it and therefore is the opposite of fire-killing.

System, subsystem: Traditionally defined as "a set of entities, real or abstract, where each entity interacts with, or is related to, at least one other entity." This set of sequentially related and linear actions and/

or events has a singular purpose. Within the *Work the System* context, we are interested in recurring systems. Note that the terms *system* and *subsystem* are interchangeable depending on context.

Tweaking: The opposite of neglect. The assertive, boots-on-the-ground mechanics of making incremental system improvements that ultimately produce hyperefficient primary systems.

Workingman's (or workingwoman's) philosophy: A set of beliefs stemming from the hard, cold, sometimes dirty realities of the job site; the view that a carefully composed blueprint directs the assembly of individual pieces into a superb end product.

Working procedures: The third of the three primary *Work the System* controlling documents. These are instructions that describe how the individual systems of the company or the job are to operate. They are end products of the system-improvement process. Written working procedures are not necessary for personal life. (See chapter 11.)

Work the System methodology: The mechanical process of establishing goals and then perfecting the systems that will help attain those goals.

Work the System mind-set: The crystal clear internal understanding of the mechanical way the things of this world operate. Typically arriving as an epiphany in a moment of time, this viewpoint makes it easy to isolate systems for examination and modification.

PART ONE

THE MIND-SET

CHAPTER 1

Control Is a Good Thing

There are some people who live in a dream world,
and there are some who face reality; and then there
are those who turn one into the other.

—Douglas Everett

For many, hearing any version of the statement "To get what you want, you must have more control" evokes the response that seeking control is a bad thing. They counter that one should relax and go with the flow, stay loose, and not worry so much about details, and that seeking more and more control can only mean one is devolving into a nervous control freak. There is an almost cosmological sense—a carryover from the '60s, perhaps—that "we're all one," and the problems in our lives and the world around us are due to people who don't share our brand of let-it-be spirituality. If my boss, my spouse, my parents, my children, my neighbor, and my government would just lighten up and be sensible—like me—then everyone could be happy!

Confident in the truth of it, we are eager to proclaim that the states of our lives—and of the world—are not good. We exhort that people are too uptight, too concerned with tiny details.

Allow me to retort.

Notwithstanding the possible metaphysical truth of the "we're all one" mantra, it's my contention that being in command of the details of our lives is mandatory if we are to find personal peace and success—if we are to find happiness. Conversely, while we're focusing on those things that are in our control, we must "lighten up" about those things that are not in our control. If we attempt to control events we can't influence, we are in for disappointment.

Is it difficult to determine what we can and cannot control? No, it's not.

My generation emphasized a great and useful truth: "What's happening now" *is* the most important thing. But I also know that the satisfaction I feel in any particular moment has much to do with the details I've managed in days past. Yes, I try hard to "be here now," but I spend some of that "here" time focusing on actions that will ensure future moments will be serene and efficient.

WALLOWING

With my younger brother as an ally, I was brought up in my grandparents' house in a small town in upstate New York. It was a chaotic, unsettled household.

At seventeen, I was on the streets of the Haight district in San Francisco. It was 1967, the Summer of Love, when I discovered an intriguing escape from the not-so-perfect family situation back home. For two years, I traveled around the country, wallowing in sex, drugs, and rock 'n' roll. (Well, maybe not that much sex.)

In the summer of '69 I ended up at the Woodstock Music and Art Fair, the famous gathering of 500,000 in rural upstate New York. *Far out*, I thought. Afterward, I continued to fruitlessly seek a better state of mind, and two more years wafted by in a blur of pot and whatever other substance was handy. I was the poster child for the freewheeling '60s.

In my self-imposed stupor there was little I didn't complain about. I tried college but dropped out my second year, distraught in my loneliness and with my vision of a world gone mad. In 1970, during a Washington, D.C., political demonstration, I was teargassed. Literally, as the mist of gas rained down on our heads, I met the woman who was to be my wife and the mother of my two children. Within weeks, with my new love in tow, I revisited the now dangerous street life of San Francisco. We lived on those streets for two months and then returned to upstate New York.

Through it all, I balked at everything that didn't align itself with my idea of rightness, chafing at the unfairness of it all. I ranted that too many selfish people were controlling things, selfish people who were conspiring to ruin my life. Of course, I was a beacon of equanimity.

In truth, I was a pain to everyone around me while my life was a series of dead-end jobs and fleeting relationships with unhappy people not unlike myself. Profoundly unhappy, I was a narcissistic complainer, haunted by self-imposed psychic hooligans.

In the middle of all this, I married my tear-gas love. Not surprisingly, my bride was equally frustrated with the unfairness of life. We were two peas in a pod, loud and bold, convinced of our rightness and everyone else's wrongness.

Then, after six years of wallowing in this fog-existence, the chains suddenly fell off one August morning in 1973. Hung over and depressed yet again, I sat at the kitchen table in the dumpy apartment I shared with my wife. I was earning minimum wage as a seasonal worker at a recreational campsite, collecting garbage and cleaning public restrooms. I was late for work that morning, but nevertheless I sat there immobile, looking inward. I declared to myself, essentially, *I'm not living like this anymore. Until now, my point of view has been wrong. No longer will I try to change the world by whining about it and fighting it. There is very little outside myself I can control, so I will stop agonizing over those things. I will arrange to go back to school this fall to learn something that can be used to create a future. From now on there will be no more complaining, no more blaming. Rather than rejecting the world as it's presented to me, I will get inside it—as it is—and see what I can do with the parts of it that are in my control.*

Little did I know that my desperate acquiescence of "the system" in my midtwenties would be the first step toward writing a book thirty-five years later that would point out the beauty of systems and the freedoms they can provide. But unlike my preoccupations back then, what I write about here has nothing to do with politics, esoteric theory, or right or wrong. It's about simple mechanics.

I enrolled at the New York State Ranger School in the Adirondack Mountains of upstate New York to study forestry and land surveying. I put my head down, worked hard through the winter, and graduated the next summer with a technical degree. Continuing to pay attention to the details, my wife and I (and our five-month-old son) headed to Oregon with $400 in our pockets and everything we owned packed into a home-made trailer attached to the back of our Plymouth. I had made a stand. I was improving my life—and the lives of the two people who were depending on me—by expending my energy only on details that I could control. The fog in my head had lifted due to an absurdly simple adjustment in my thinking process.

But despite those first positive steps at dealing with the real world by focusing on what was truly in my control, I had not yet recognized the next necessary "systems-perspective" step that would lead to actually getting the peace and prosperity I wanted. In this ignorance, I would carry some very heavy baggage for another twenty-five years.

PERPETUAL DISAPPOINTMENT

The best illustration of the baggage I carried is a photo taken at Woodstock. It's one you may have seen. It's of a lovely, slender, long-haired girl who is maybe eighteen years old. She's beautiful, and she's dancing in a meadow in a long, sheer dress. There is a flower wreath in her hair and she's laughing as she whirls with her arms stretched above her head in a casual way. Her thin, handsome, ponytailed boyfriend is dancing, too. They share a blissful peace-joy ecstasy, and anyone who sees that photo would, at least for a moment, want to be one of those two young people.

The image is a declaration of pure bliss with the clear message that unrestrained freedom and happiness are attainable, and the path to that place requires no more than a carefree and unrestrained comportment, hip music, and an unlimited supply of drugs. With a broad metaphorical brushstroke, the message of that photo is that happiness is available as soon as we drop our uptight preoccupations and "dance in the meadow." Let it all hang out. Stay loose. Go with the flow.

Back to the real world. The photo is an enticement for a state of mind that exists only for brief moments. Its message is a sham. One can't just "lighten up" and then expect ongoing happiness. Life isn't that way. But many of us who evolved from that era think it should be that way, and so we live from day to day in perpetual disappointment, within a world that won't conform to our expectations. Forty years after the '60s, that silly perspective has carried over to our children and beyond. We share a culture of chronic disappointment, and it's no surprise that many of us are crass, self-absorbed, and narcissistic. We bask in wealth the world has never known but wonder why our lives are chaotic and why we are unsatisfied.

We obsess about our yearning states of mind as we grope for personal peace. (Don't get me wrong as I make my points here. I don't like focusing on negatives, and this is a bit painful for me as I discuss the unhappy contortions of my generation. But it's a necessary discussion for understanding the *Work the System* premise, so I have to start here—in the negative—in order to set the stage for the rest of the book, which I promise you will find uplifting.)

DANCING-IN-THE-MEADOW SYNDROME

In the Western world, 10 percent of adults are alcoholics, 70 percent drink copious amounts of caffeine, 25 percent are addicted to tobacco, and more than 10 percent rely on antidepressants. Throw in the other legal and illegal mood-altering drugs and it is safe to say that each day, 98 percent of us ingest at least one mood-altering substance in our endless search for better states of mind. Of course, many of us are multi-substance users, for instance, consuming caffeine in the morning and alcohol at night. One substance counters the negative effects of the other in the classic, endless loop of Western chemical mood adjustment.

The Price to Be Paid

Abusing personal systems too often means introducing medications into the miraculous near-perfect system that is the body. Perceiving themselves to be unhappy, people complicate their already flawed thinking process by contaminating themselves. The ice-cold reality? One plus one always equals two, and with the same utter reliability, a drunken night out on the town equals days of subpar physical and mental performance as the human body works overtime to repair itself from the chemical assault. Too often, we make things worse in the long term by violating systems in the short term, as we ignore the simple truth that disruption of an efficient system always has its price. One could say that substance abuse is a criminal attack against one's self.

So we finger-point and complain and wonder at our dissatisfaction. It's too bad we do that because it's not just a waste of time, it's a diversion from what needs to happen in order to find life satisfaction. Personal excuses, generalizations about the alleged dire state of the world, and under-the-radar as well as overt attempts to change the people around us are ineffectual to the point of paralysis. These preoccupations are distractions from the personal actions we could take that would produce what we want in our individual lives: peace, prosperity, and control of our destinies. And pursuing personal peace, prosperity, and control are noble goals because the sure way to realize them is to contribute to the people around us.

What about the generally accepted notion that someone who seeks firm control is an unpleasant personality, someone who needs to loosen up? With some rare exceptions, I submit that this ubiquitous assumption is wrong.

Despite the almost visceral societal belief to the contrary, *there is a direct connection between happiness and the amount of control we attain.*

But let's be clear: Happiness is not found in the control we have over others. It's found in the control we have over the moment-to-moment trajectory of our own lives, and more exactly—here we get to the root of things—the control of the personal systems that are ours to adjust and maintain.

The solution to getting what we want and making a contribution is not in complaining about the world condition or ingesting the perfect drug.

And it's not about acquiring more things or being popular or famous. The solution is rooted in adopting a different perspective—a different way of seeing, thinking, and processing things—and it's about facing the world cold-turkey, courageously questioning the sacred status quo as it relates to our own selves. It's about sorting out what's going on within our individual areas of direct influence.

The thinking process is a linear system, and my contention, as illustrated in the dancing girl photo, is that many of us make a fundamental error in executing that process. Albeit tongue in cheek, I like to call this chronic thinking error the "Dancing-in-the-Meadow Syndrome."

Your Circle of Influence

A metaphorical concept made popular by Stephen Covey, the circle of influence describes one's ability to have an impact in life. In years past, I was hardly able to influence and control my own comings and goings due to whatever psychological funk was swallowing me up in the moment. My circle of influence felt like it was maybe two feet in diameter. Now, my circle feels as if it's miles in diameter as my days effortlessly sail by and I am able to accomplish nearly all that I set out to accomplish. This impact gives me enormous satisfaction as the wheels of progress keep turning due to my previous input, not because of my immediate presence.

Take a moment to use your imagination and describe your own circle. How large is it? Is it just six inches in diameter? If it is, when you look down, is the six-inch circle hidden underneath your feet? If the tiny circle was even twelve inches in diamerter, you could barely balance on it. Do you spend all your available energy and attention just trying not to fall off? If that is your situation, your tenuous balancing effort doesn't leave much time for anything but complaining.

Wherever you are, whatever the size of your circle of influence, focus on making changes inside of it, not outside. Don't spend precious time and energy analyzing and dissecting big-picture issues you cannot affect. Instead, spend that time and energy on the things you *can* affect, things within your circle. Do that, and your circle will expand.

LIFE IS A STREAMING VIDEO, NOT A SNAPSHOT

Outside of brief moments within that encapsulated era, the unbridled approach of the '60s was just another great idea that didn't work. It was a theory that didn't consider how we are but how we thought we should be. If the Woodstock meadow-dancing photo had instead been a documentary movie, the hours and days surrounding that dance would tell a different story.

The truth of Woodstock? The nonstop music was good, but few bands played their best due to the confusion and pervasive drug ingestion. Yes, it was peaceful, but after that first glorious day, it was cold and wet, and we sat in the mud shivering, drenched, hungry, and thirsty. In the rain, a half million of us worked hard to relax, insistent in our success at being together outside "the system" for nothing more than music and love. "It's all we need!" we told ourselves over and over again. We had jumped outside the everyday world, but in our T-shirts, jeans, and little else, we were unprepared as the chilly torrent hammered down. It was no contest as soft theory met bare-knuckled hard reality.

With the inevitability of a wave washing into shore, the enthusiasm faded as the filth that comes with neglected crowds began to accumulate. After two days of this, as a general paranoia swept through the wet, shivering, drug-addled horde, my friend John and I got out of there. We left before Jimi Hendrix had taken the stage. It was that bad.

As we headed home in my beat-up wreck of a car, listening to the radio, we were reminded of Vietnam, racial unrest, and political deviousness. And beyond those negatives, we both worked graveyard shifts in a paper mill, and as we drove north, exhausted and depressed, any joy we experienced at Woodstock was within a narrow sliver in time.

John was eighteen years old; I was nineteen. We were college-dropout party guys and proud of our chaotic lifestyles. We never thought of the relationship between our self-absorbed, uncontrolled lives and our unhappiness. As I think back and make judgments, it occurs to me the ones who were creating something worthwhile were the "straight" kids. They were not immune to down times, but in their willingness to conform to the reality of the world, they were more in control and, yes, happier.

The lure of dancing in the meadow is an invitation to illusionary bliss. Truth is, orderliness and attention to detail are the roots of peace. Proof? Consider the indisputable reverse logic: In any setting, the opposite of peace—disorder—always leads to desperation. It's this way for any out-of-control situation: a natural disaster, riot, car accident, or family argument. The outcome is never a pretty sight.

Too many of us are paralyzed in the static snapshot of how we think things should be instead of working with the mechanics of the world as it is. Life is not a snapshot; it's a real-time, streaming video—and the video plays on whether we participate in it or not.

DISTRACTED

So, forty years later, what is the relevance? For those who still buy into the '60s mystique, an unfounded assumption smolders. It whispers there is chaos all around, that systems and organization are bad, and that Big Brother is right there behind the curtain, steering things in the wrong direction.

This thread of paranoia leaves too many of us obsessing about things that are out of our control, and the obsessing distracts us from taking the actions that would truly make us free! It's not "the system" that holds us back; it's the flaw in our perception. As we focus on the events outside ourselves that we cannot control, we overlook the imperfect aspects of our own lives that we can control. We don't recognize that recurring personal pain is not often the result of a flawed world, but more usually the result of our own flawed personal systems—systems we can repair! We don't grasp that experiencing peace and prosperity—nothing less than freedom—comes from paying strict attention to the details of our own lives.

If we don't overtly take control of the forward flow of our own lives, the mistake of a lifetime is just around the corner, ready to flatten us when we least expect it. More endemic and less dramatic, small inefficiencies will take us to the same dark place. Life carries on whether we like it or not, and this churning flow is at our command only if we pay close attention to the details.

Back in 1974, as my family and I moved west, what I still didn't under-stand was that the mind-set of the people who are successful in life, the people who create and build and contribute—the ones who have poise, freedom, and wealth—is to pay attention to the mechanical details of life. I didn't understand that peace and prosperity arrive *after* the mechanics are in order. This requires forethought, organization, and rational thinking, and that means well-attended systems. The way of the world is mechanical!

A DEARTH OF SYSTEMS

From a systems perspective, what happened at Woodstock? One system that worked well was the system that delivered the music. The technicians were adept and the equipment functioned adequately. The musicians showed up, which meant the transportation system worked—the entertainers were delivered by helicopter. The location (Yasgur's farm) worked.

What systems did not work? Outside of the above, you name it: The ticketing system failed, with all the surrounding fences coming down early in the process—a disaster for the promoters who sponsored the event. The sanitation and medical systems were overwhelmed and borderline dysfunctional. If overt police protection had been required, it would have been mayhem because there was little more than a tiny contingent of informal private security guards.

Of course, from a personal systems perspective, few in the audience were physically prepared, even in a rudimentary way. To compound things, drug use was hampering rational thinking. Everyone was in the middle of everything, and chaos was a breadth away, held back by no more than the luck of the draw.

One day of peace and music? Yes, okay, that's true. Two days? Well, the drugs helped maintain a certain calmness, but things were stretched. Three days? Whew! It was an exodus out of there! If there had been four days? For those diehards who might have remained, it would have been a sordid, nasty affair.

It was the love and goodwill of the people that made the festival work. But that sliver of "bliss-time" was narrow and can't serve as an example of how a life can be lived day to day. "I love you, man" is not enough for the long term.

A Potent, Visceral Reminder from the Folks at NASA

A space shuttle is arguably the most complex machine ever built by man, and a launch is perhaps the most magnificent display of human system control. I never miss an opportunity to watch the event on TV in real time.

The next time you watch a launch, consider the precision of the countdown, which relies on thousands of simultaneous and automatic monitoring processes, all overseen by engineers and technicians. The launch executes, and tens of thousands of active systems, both on the craft and on the ground, execute independently and in concert, each a precision entity unto itself.

As of the publication date of this book, there have been 125 flights, 2 of which were spectacularly horrible failures. Yet, considering the incredible complexity of the endeavor, and acknowledging the human penchant for error, one could legitimately wonder why there have not been more catastrophes than this.

Like countless minor failures of the past, these tragedies provide space shuttle engineers with information they can use to prevent future problems. As time moves on, the chances of minor and major failure decrease steadily as the space shuttle system is tweaked ever closer to perfection.

As you watch the next liftoff—the keynote celebration of human potential, and a potent, visceral illustration of the beauty of the countless systems that comprise our existences—consider the following question while you marvel at the miracle: *Could space shuttle system improvements—most of which are based on advancements in science, engineering, and mathematics, but many of which are based on previous failure—be the result of an outside and slightly elevated vantage point?*

CHAPTER 2

A System of Systems

King Arthur (Graham Chapman) (after cutting off both of the Black Knight's arms): *Look, you stupid bastard. You've got no arms left!*
Black Knight (John Cleese): *Yes I have! . . . It's just a flesh wound!*

—FROM THE MOVIE *MONTY PYTHON AND THE HOLY GRAIL* (EMI FILMS, 1975)

ONE REASON I USE CENTRATEL TO ILLUSTRATE the *Work the System* framework is that it is an easily understood "primary" system that is composed of subsystems. That is, Centratel is a closed "system-of-systems." It provides simple, real-world, cause-and-effect depictions of the principles. As I go through the details, you will be able to read between the lines and understand how the picture I paint is also applicable to all aspects of your life, not just your business/work environment. It applies directly to your own most important system-of-systems: you.

CENTRATEL OVERVIEW

For fifteen years Centratel struggled for survival, always at the brink of disaster. Why did this system of systems begin to prosper in year sixteen? Yes, focused attention, terrific staff, targeted marketing, and a consistently high-quality product went a long way, but they were not the cause of the turnaround. Instead, these were the by-products of the cause. The root cause of the turnaround was the discovery and application of the principle that management must focus on improving systems, not in performing the work or in repeatedly snuffing out brushfires. In short, quality products or services, a stable staff, and profitability are the *result* of the quality systems that produce them, not the reverse.

Centratel is a high-tech, national telephone answering service. As I write this, our gross yearly revenues are approaching $3 million. As a third-party "outsourced" business, a telephone answering service (TAS) employs telephone service representatives (TSRs) who process incoming telephone calls (from "callers") for various businesses (clients). Essentially a private 911 service, any answering service's purpose is to take messages from the client's callers and then deliver those messages to the client. Clients include medical and veterinary clinics, funeral homes, property management companies, HVAC operations, high-tech firms, and the like. These are businesses that must provide 24/7/365 human interaction to their customers or patients. Since these businesses can't cover their phones 24/7, they must employ an answering service to screen and process after-hours calls. A smaller group of clients uses an answering service during daytime hours when incoming phone traffic is more than they can handle, or if they don't have a physical office.

At Centratel, up to twelve TSRs (depending on call traffic) sit at work-stations and field one call after another, with the incoming calls arriving randomly from any one of approximately nine hundred accounts. Some-times when traffic is heavy, calls come in like machine-gun fire. One call will be from a nervous husband whose wife is on the way to the hospital to have a baby; the next call from the panicked owner of a horse that has colic; the next from an apartment tenant who has accidentally locked her-self out of her apartment. You get the idea.

Our TSRs take messages, record them in a database, and then deliver them in a variety of ways including pager, cell phone, voice mailbox, e-mail, or fax. It is an unbelievably complex enterprise, with multitudes of human and mechanical systems working simultaneously. Caller, client, and TSR communication is constant and nearly always time sensitive. At Centratel, each of our accounts provides unique and exact instructions on how to handle callers and process messages. So within any TAS business there is enormous opportunity for error, and without strict system proto-col and superior staff, it's an understatement to say it's a breeding ground for chaos.

The TAS industry stretches back to the first days of telephones. As they were then, answering services are now: nonstop operations. This all-the-time activity engenders another interesting challenge: odd working hours for TSRs as they come and go from the office at all times of the day and night. It can be a tough way to earn a living, a major personal challenge for those who work the after-hours schedules. Our more senior TSRs have worked themselves into traditional daytime shifts, but new people must earn their stripes, enduring the tougher schedules until they can move into better slots that open due to staff attrition and company expansion. In any case, the pay and benefits are very good at Centratel, close to double industry averages.

It's a fascinating industry, but it is in decline. In 1975, the total number of TAS businesses in the United States was more than twenty thousand, most of which were small mom-and-pop operations. Now, survivors are larger—but perhaps only two thousand total—and as a percentage of the overall population, the number of TAS clients has also decreased considerably. Cell phones, pagers, voice mail, the Internet, and telephone company switching options have cut deeply into the industry. Nevertheless, plenty of businesses still require a real-live human being to process their incoming calls, and the market will not be disappearing any time soon.

More than two decades ago, I contemplated entering the TAS business for three reasons (and these reasons are still good general considerations for anyone going into business).

First, it intrigued me that it was all about people and communication.

Second, revenues would be passive. If managed properly, I would not have to be physically present in order to receive income. I was young and new to business, but it seemed to me that making money without having to show up to do the work would beat being a doctor, attorney, teacher, psychologist, working man, or any number of occupations where a specific individual is the centerpiece of the endeavor.

Third, revenues would be recurring—clients would continuously use our services and pay us over and over again. With clients paying monthly, generating new income would not be a full-time, daily challenge. I reasoned that if the product was superior and our clients were happy, the money would constantly flow.

So on December 1, 1984, at the age of thirty-five, I bought Girl Friday Telephone Answering Service, an ailing TAS in my hometown of Bend, Oregon. The total purchase price was $21,000; the down payment, $5,000. There were seven employees, 140 clients, and 400 square feet of office space.

Now the owner of a business, I changed the name of the company to reflect the changing times, and—per my arrogant cockiness in those days—announced to anyone who would listen that we would someday be the highest-quality telephone answering service in the United States. Despite my bravado, I had no idea how we would achieve such a goal. (As I think back on those days and how I went about things, the words "brash" and "clueless" enter my mind.)

Events did not unfold as anticipated. The business was a disorganized nightmare, and my personal life, what there was of it, devolved into shambles. Within a year, I went through a divorce and then proceeded to do my best to bring up my two children as a single, custodial parent.

Although always on the brink of disaster, Centratel grew in volume—but profits never increased. It was an epic struggle, and as the first years passed, the "Best in the U.S." goal disappeared behind the cloud of chaos.

For a decade and a half, I endured moment-to-moment turmoil, working long, long hours—often in excess of a hundred hours a week—always just scratching by financially. I got sick from the pressure but powered on anyway. The only thing that would stop me would be if I dropped over unconscious from stress and sheer fatigue (and after fifteen years of relentless pressure, this became more than a possibility).

Then, as previously mentioned, I had an unforeseen insight and began to apply the *Work the System* principles to my business and my personal life. An earthmoving event, the new vision deeply affected me, subtly yet profoundly changing the way I perceived the world. With this new outlook, all aspects of my life improved as the turbulence subsided. It became a different world at Centratel and at home.

Just after my "enlightenment," I brought a partner into the business—a good man, an acquaintance I had always respected—and I was no longer in it alone. Now I had a second set of professional eyes, and with his stock purchase, a financial boost. Coincidentally, my partner's name is Sam, too.

The next few chapters describe the odyssey in detail. As you read, think of parallels in your own life.

 ## Installing a Preventative System

Sometimes we install a system and it doesn't do much. We achieve the desired effect by the mere existence of it. At Centratel, we knew that a few of our employees spent time "cruising the net" on company time. It was impossible to track these sleight-of-hand excursions, and the closest we could get to managing the problem was to walk around a corner and find a staff member covertly closing a non-Centratel window upon our approach.

So we installed special software that tracks and logs Internet activity. The software solved the problem instantly and completely. We track everyone's activity, including who goes where and how much time is spent Web surfing.

Have we ever tracked down bad behavior with it? Yes, when we first installed the software without announcing what we had done, the usual suspects emerged. Did we say anything to them? No, it wasn't necessary because we knew that once we announced the installation and noted it in our Employee Handbook, the people who were abusing the system would change their behavior. Did they? Yes. Have we had subsequent abuses? No. We carefully check the logs each month, but there is never a problem.

In our culture, other examples of preventative systems include drug testing, the police, and laws. The systems are intended to halt problems before they occur.

Think of preventative systems in your personal life: the seat belts in your car that don't just protect you from injury but remind you that a defensive driving posture is paramount; the routine backups on your computer; the small courtesies you show to loved ones and strangers alike. As you go through your day, think of systems you can implement that will prevent problems down the line.

What steps do you take to protect your child or your pet or your household belongings? What processes does the federal government maintain in order to keep conflicts from occurring?

CHAPTER 3
The Attack of the Moles

Gwen DeMarco (Sigourney Weaver): *They are so cute!*

Guy Fleegman (Sam Rockwell): *Sure, they're cute now, but in a second they're gonna get mean, and they're gonna get ugly somehow, and there's gonna be a million more of them.*

—FROM THE MOVIE *GALAXY QUEST* (DREAMWORKS, 1999)

ALL ANSWERING SERVICES PERFORM THE SAME FUNCTION for their clients, and my newly purchased TAS was no exception. At all hours of the day and night, our TSRs took incoming calls from our clients' callers. When clients called in, the TSRs read the written messages back to them. It was the mid-1980s when, for much of the business world, word processing and computer database management were little more than future concepts. We were a mom-and-pop service, and for a "flat rate" of $35 to $45 per month, we processed as many calls as the client could send us. During the day, two TSRs handled calls; after hours, one.

From the beginning and for fifteen subsequent years, I managed all aspects of the operation myself. From the first day of ownership, it was a madhouse because most of our clients had taken advantage of the flat-rate arrangement and used our TSRs as their full-time telephone reception-ists. Our staff were overwhelmed with call traffic and so the quality of call handling was abysmal. At first, because I had no understanding of the internal mechanics of the answering service business, all I could do was watch and wonder.

When I bought the business, the monthly total gross revenue of $5,500 was not enough to cover wages, rent, telephone company costs, and everything else including supporting myself and my two children. The business had been mine for only two months and disaster was already at hand. ("Disaster at hand" was to become a serial catchphrase over the ensuing years.) Standing by without taking action would be a quick ticket to failure, so with my staff, and my eight- and ten-year-olds depending on me, I had to do something immediately. Here, my brashness would be useful.

It was a fortunate irony that the business was in terrible shape when I bought it—some positive aspects lay hidden. After just a few weeks the major problems were obvious even to me, someone with zero knowledge of the industry. It was clear I must immediately correct the most glaring inefficiency: a customer-pricing schedule that was too low. The fortunate part was that our service rates were extremely low—we could raise them significantly and still remain competitive.

I informed our clients by letter that service rates were going up and we would start charging for the actual call traffic we handled for their individual accounts. I told them a large price hike was the only choice if we were to stay in business. So we dropped the flat-rate billing plan and began counting message slips, billing each account for actual messages processed by TSRs.

On average, this *tripled* our customers' costs, and immediately one-third of them terminated service, while others cut down the call traffic forwarded to us. The decrease in incoming call traffic allowed our TSRs to spend more time on each call, and because they were less rushed, the quality of service improved—the first of many incremental quality improvements that were to accumulate over the years ahead.

As a sidelight, and to illustrate just how low our service rates had been, even with the 300 percent increase, our prices remained lower than our much larger local TAS competitor.

Despite losing more than 30 percent of our total client base, monthly revenues doubled overnight to $11,000. The huge increase in income was terrific, but equipment had to be upgraded and wages raised. So even with the additional cash boost, the company was still not profitable. We raised rates again in six months and then again six months after that. One year later we did it again. Nonetheless, we continued to struggle.

This just-barely-hanging-on predicament endured. Over the next decade and a half, we couldn't get ahead even though we managed to multiply gross receipts by a factor of twelve. Our revenue growth was due to rate increases as well as the new clients we gained because of our growing reputation for quality—quality that had risen from terrible to marginal (but marginal quality was better than our local competitor who remained at the "terrible" level because of their own self-perpetuated chaos). The rise in income was always matched by increases in operating costs. The largest increases were in wages, health insurance, retirement, and other benefits to the TSR staff.

Within three years, we moved to a larger office space. We stayed in that location for twelve years and then moved to an even larger space. We continued to grow, but the turmoil and cash flow problems increased.

For a decade and a half, my small salary didn't change while my 80–100-hour workweeks continued unabated. I had no life outside the business, and any personal time went to my children.

As the years passed, I learned the ropes and prided myself on being expert at every facet of the business, able to perform any function. Within moments, I could move from scheduling staff, to handling customer complaints, to solving telephone company problems. I could interview a job applicant for a TSR position one minute and in the next put together a plan for adding a computer system. I could prepare payroll while I signed up a new account and then head to the bank to plead my case for yet another small loan. I did it all including being there as the single parent of my kids (the task-juggling at home rivaled the task-juggling at the office).

What a feeling of power as I simultaneously solved multiple problems. I was a master of survival-juggling, a fire-killer extraordinaire! How heroic! But in my arrogance, and swept up in the endless fire-killing, I was spinning my wheels and headed for destruction.

THIS SURVIVAL THING IS KILLING ME

With the exception of whatever happened to be going on in my mind on any given day, there was no direction for the company. Centratel grew because of a booming local economy and my knack for foiling the reaper at the last minute.

Through those years, I single-handedly fixed whatever needed to be fixed, smoothed out the rough spots, and kept the ball rolling no matter the day of the week or time of the day. Long-term planning didn't happen and routine maintenance was no more than a vague concept for the future.

The Numbers Are Gloomy

Statistics show that of one hundred new business start-ups, only twenty will remain after five years. Then, in the next five years, four of those remaining twenty will still be functioning. In another five years, three of those four will disappear, leaving one out of the original hundred. That's a 99 percent small business fatality rate over a fifteen-year period.

Gauge your own situation and look ahead. Are you an employee of a small business? If so, the numbers are not on your side. Or do you own a small business? If so, there is hope because you have the power to direct it.

Too often, what ends a business or a job, or what casts an onerous spell on a life, is "death by a thousand cuts." This is relentless erosion caused by recurring inefficiencies and their offspring: fire-killing and distraction. These time wasters undermine efforts to create and sell a good product that has a viable market. And in personal life? You've seen it in those who can't seem to break out of the bad-luck syndrome. For business or personal life, it's not mysterious bad luck that takes people down; it's serial inefficiency. The great news is that inefficiency is easy to correct if one can see the cause of it.

As the ten-year anniversary passed, my days spiraled downward into ever-deepening chaos. I leaped from one predicament to the next as crises multiplied. The days were crammed with cash flow crunches, chronic staff absenteeism, and innumerable customer complaints. The office temperature was too cool—or too warm. We would run out of critical office supplies and not have the time to leave the office to replace them. Turnover among TSRs was incessant, and scheduling was haphazard, put together at the last moment. In year ten, we went through more than sixty new people—and my total number of staff was twelve! TSR trainees would start work, stay for a week, and quit. My employees were unhappy, and the same held true for our clients as they endured a still marginal quality of service.

Making payroll was always a challenge: every two weeks it was a last-minute, hold-your-breath epic as we gambled that all payroll checks would clear. Twice they didn't, and I went to employees' homes with cash to cover their bounced checks, pleading with them to give me another chance and come back to work.

I was the heroic jack-of-all-trades, the master fire-killer who would work as long and as hard as necessary.

The years drifted by. My teenagers would wait for me at home as I flailed around at the office late into the night. When I finally came home, I would check to see if they were sleeping okay, and then stumble into my bedroom and climb into bed. I would lie there exhausted with that deep, deep fatigue way down inside the chest.

Bills were not paid on time, both at Centratel and at home. Collectors called day and night. Checks bounced, and NSF fees accumulated, sometimes over $100 at a time. The people at the bank felt sorry for me as they marveled at both my endurance and my ineptitude in keeping the money straight.

For a while, my two teenagers shared the office space with me because we could not afford a place to live. They went to school during the day and at night slept on bunk beds in the back room of Centratel's small office. When I could, I slept alongside them on a cot.

Then, after the kids had gone off to college, in one long stretch of seven months, I answered calls as the sole TSR on the midnight to 8:00 a.m. shift every night. Here's the kicker: During those seven months, Monday through Friday of every week, I also worked in the daytime from 8:00 a.m. to 5:00 p.m., taking care of 100 percent of the administrative and management tasks. This meant each weekday my shift began at midnight and ended no sooner than 5:00 p.m. the next day. Weekends were a relief because I only had to work the midnight to 8:00 a.m. shifts. My workweek exceeded a hundred hours. Of course, there was no social life. I didn't have time for friends.

During those months I was sleeping just a few hours each night and never in a single stretch because, as the sole midnight TSR, I had to wake up each time a call came into the service. Throughout the shift, the medical and veterinary emergency calls came in at a steady pace. Lying on the floor with a pillow and blanket, there was the occasional straight hour of sleep. After my seven-month stretch of graveyard shifts, when I fell back to my normal eighty-hour workweeks, it was impossible to sleep through the night even when there was the opportunity. My body had become hardwired to perform a day's work with three hours of sleep.

I wondered how soon my physical and/or mental collapse would occur, but there was no relief due to my intimate involvement with every aspect of the operation. The business would immediately fail if I wasn't there moment-to-moment.

For the body and the mind, few things are worse than long-term sleep deprivation, and eventually I succumbed to the stress. It was a depression and exhaustion that inhibited every thought and action. My performance became clumsy in the face of escalating problems. Things were getting worse by the day, and after fifteen years of accumulated trauma, the end was near.

If things were so bad, why didn't I throw in the towel and get a regular job? I was terrified of rejoining the workforce as someone's employee. The thought of having a traditional job sent shivers down my spine. After all those years of being on my own, working for someone else would be a nightmare for me *and* for my employer. I rationalized, if I am in Hell, at least it's *my* Hell.

PLAYING A GAME I COULDN'T WIN

I had no idea what to do other than what I had always done, to dig in and take care of whatever came up. It was horrible and the fire-killing got worse. I kept at it. My existence was like the Whac-A-Mole game in which little grinning-faced moles keep popping their heads up in any one of a dozen holes. I would whack one mole and two more would emerge. My hammer would respond in a flurry and the mole heads would be rammed back down into their tunnels, one after the other. It was a beautiful performance, a remarkable demonstration of dexterity and power.

The Whac-A-Mole Game, per Wikipedia

According to Wikipedia,

> Once the game starts, the moles pop up from their holes at random. The object of the game is to force the individual moles back into their holes by hitting them directly on the head with the mallet, thereby adding to the player's score. If the player does not strike a mole within a certain time or with enough force, it will eventually sink back into its hole with no score. Although game play starts out slow enough for most people to hit all of the moles that rise, it gradually increases in speed, with each mole spending less time above the hole and with more moles outside of their holes at the same time. After a designated time limit, the game ends, regardless of the skill of the player. The final score is based upon the number of moles the player struck.

But despite the heroics, the mole whacking was distracting me from seeing what was necessary to fix my business and my life. Centratel's daily disaster control was diverting me from facing the reality that I was playing a game that should not be played—a game I could never win.

 ## Jim Morrison and Mick Jagger

Morrison and Jagger are arguably the best lead singers rock has ever produced: Morrison's voice and lyrics, Jagger's voice and flair. Jim Morrison's short, wild ride was fueled by his brilliant observations and brazen thought-images, built around a mystique of chaos. He wallowed in the haunting darkness and wondered about the great unknown beyond death. He lived in chaos, too, awash in alcohol and drugs, abusing his physical and mental systems. He died at the age of twenty-seven after just four years of performing and recording. His too-short life was the antith-esis of systemization and order.

Mick Jagger, however, has been hammering away for better than forty-five years, ten times longer than did Morrison. Essentially, Jagger is general manager and CEO of the Rolling Stones, personally attending to the operation of the band's enormously sophisticated and complex tour-ing/recording machine. He is as fit as any twenty-five-year-old, eschewing drugs and alcohol. Whether it's creating music, performing, recording, or managing the enormous complexity that is his world, system improvement is clearly his primary aim. Enormously talented, healthy, and wealthy, a connoisseur of antiques and art, he is a master of systemizing, tweaking, and maintaining.

Is there something you do to your body that is making it less efficient? Are you excelling in system management in some areas while sabotaging yourself in others?

CHAPTER 4

Gun-to-the-Head Enlightenment

It is often darkest just before dawn.

—SOJOURNER TRUTH

FOR FIFTEEN YEARS I POUNDED MY SMALL BUSINESS into some kind of subservient yet mocking submission, carrying on like a perpetual motion machine. But, of course, it was tenuous. Everything depended on me, and if I let up for one moment, my world would come crashing down. It was just a matter of time.

Then, on the heels of my seven-month double-shift epic, I hit a brick wall. In my arsenal of last-minute bailout strategies, there was no solution to the deathblow crisis looming just ahead—the inability to cover the next payroll. On payday, my staff would walk out when there were no paychecks, instantly ending my business as our clients raced elsewhere to find another answering service to handle their calls. In a single moment, Centratel would close its doors and everything I had accomplished in the past decade and a half would be lost, not to mention that my staff of sixteen would be jobless and my three hundred loyal clients would be in crisis.

I was a mentally and physically wrecked fifty-year-old single parent facing financial and career oblivion, and it was more than an interesting coincidence the imminent end of Centratel was dovetailing with my almost certain mental and/or physical breakdown. I was desperate—and for the first time, angry—and the doomsday clock was ticking.

DAWN

The payroll was less than a week away when, yet again lying awake in bed late one night, exhausted, I stopped thinking about work details, business philosophies, elaborate theories, or some last-minute divine intervention. It was the end, and there was nothing left to examine or ruminate about, nothing left to salvage—except one small thing. In a last gesture of raw defiance, at least I could end things with some self-respect. As a final, last-gasp effort, I would either save myself or go down in a blinding flash. This would not end with a whimper. Since everything was lost anyway, why not find one last moment of control?

I lay there in the 3:00 a.m. darkness, reviewing the blinding-flash possibilities. But something was odd. I was at peace for the first time in years. How could that be? Without coaxing, and for no apparent reason, two simple, pragmatic questions charged out of the blackness: *What have I been doing wrong all these years?* and *Since the end is coming, what is there to lose if I abandon past assumptions and look at things from a completely different angle?*

My "what is there to lose" posture was the catalyst. The certain end of Centratel opened my perception gates and gave me the freedom to consider anything. No matter how outrageous, any new idea was an option because there was no further possible downside. I had a few more days to stretch into unknown territory and do some experimentation, because . . . what did it matter?

Then, answers came.

I underwent an enlightenment of sorts. It sounds corny, but in my mind, I rose up and out of the jumble that was my life; I was no longer an integral part of it. Floating upward, "outside and slightly elevated" from the chaos, I gazed down at the details of my business, spread out neatly as if on display on a tabletop. From this bird's-eye perspective, it struck me that Centratel was simply a self-contained mechanical device! It was—and is—nothing more than the sum of an assemblage of sequential systems: answering the phones, sales, payroll preparation, scheduling, handling complaints, etc.—each executed in a linear fashion whereby one step follows another step until the sequence for that particular system is complete. Instinctively, I knew the rest of my life operated in the same way: as an assemblage of separate and independent systems, occurring in predictable, reliable sequences according to their own individual construction. (Yes, I thought, of course these systems intermingle and affect each other—a holistic assemblage to be sure—but that holism can't mask the separateness of them, the beauty of their individuality.)

My thoughts raced at light speed as I marveled at the simple beauty of it. I understood that my previous vision of the world had been wrong. The world is not a chaotic jumble of people, objects, and events clanging together in disarray. The world is a place of order and logic, a place of predictability. The world is a collection of logical systems!

For the first time, I saw Centratel as an enclosed package—an independent, "primary system"—a separate entity, like a human body, an airplane, a tree, or a city. And the primary system called Centratel shared a commonality with all other primary systems in that it was the product of the sum of the myriad separate subsystems that composed it. The logic of it was crystal clear, exquisite.

A line from an old rock song by The Fixx went round and round in my head as I lay there: "One thing leads to another. One thing leads to another . . ." I looked down and saw that my mode of thinking and managing had been reactionary, defensive, and incredibly inefficient. *I had taken the wrong stance because the mechanics had been invisible to me!* All I did was kill fires, unaware that they were the products of invisible, dysfunctional subsystems. These subsystems had lives of their own and were acting out their 1-2-3 sequences without direction, producing results that were unpredictable at the least, and debilitating at the worst. *My business was out of control because I had been coping with the random products of uncontrolled systems.* My life was chaos not because I was some kind of loser or unfortunate victim of circumstance but because many of the subsystems of my life were not being managed. Out of control, these inefficient subsystems composed the dysfunctional primary systems of my life: business, health, and relationships.

WHO IS IN CHARGE OF ALL THIS?

Exhausted yet exhilarated, I lay in bed floating above it all, looking down on things, savoring the delicious new vision. It was borderline mystical, a sort of near-death experience, but without the tunnel and bright light. For the first time it was clear that my previous perception of reality had been murky and undefined. How does the saying go: "One thing I know: Once I was blind but now I see"?

From depths beyond my physical and mental despair, and liberated from my self-absorption, more questions surfaced, ones I had never considered before: *"Who is in charge of all this?"* and *"How does this world continue to function day after day, year after year, millennium after millennium?"* The answers to these odd questions came fast and hard.

I was startled to grasp that there is no human "King of Everything" who directs the goings-on of the world. On its own, and no matter what, this earth keeps turning and life carries on in an overall structured and organized pattern, and . . . *no one is in charge!* The indomitable laws of nature ensure systems work perfectly according to their construction: On this earth, gravity works all the time, everywhere. Over here, one plus one equals two, and over there, one plus one also equals two! The laws of nature cause the mechanics of the world to be dependable and predictable, and the gift with which we humans have been blessed is the ability to get in the middle of it all and to manipulate it, to direct our lives to be what we want them to be, to use the laws of nature to our advantage. *And no single human, or group of humans, is in charge!*

I floated in my thoughts and wondered at the silent, invisible background organizational strength that keeps things chugging ahead like a train, despite our human race's best attempts to derail the process. Cyclically, methodically, and for whatever reason, this complex world moves along on its own, adjusting, balancing, and counterbalancing. And at the root of it all, and in the middle of it all, uncountable separate linear systems are at work.

THE WORLD IS 99.9 PERCENT EFFICIENT

This systems rationale is not another feel-good, think-positive invocation, and it's not about faith. It's about stone-cold mechanical reality. Think about the systems of our lives and then do the numbers. We wake, shower, dress, eat, go to work, and proceed through the day to return to our loved ones in the evening. Then we watch TV, read, and go to bed early—or stay up late. We go to sleep, and then we awake again the next morning. Everything works fine 99.9 percent of the time.

That's the cursory overview. Break it down and sequentially note the other events of the day's chronology. It will be thousands of items long as it includes contributing components such as the coffee maker that works every morning; the car that—despite all of its internal intricacies—operates with the turn of a key and then the turn of the wheel; the office we occupy; the complexities of the work we do; the paychecks we receive for doing that work. Consider the process of sharing information back and forth with those around us: one-on-one, voice mail, cellular phone, e-mail, the written word. Each is a system, and 99.9 percent of the time each works flawlessly!

Envision the system we call TV: By simply pushing a button when we want to watch it, this incredibly complex mechanism jumps to life every time! Beyond the physical TV itself, consider the myriad organizations that put together the programming that appears on it. Then, switch gears and think about the lawn mower, the water that flows from the kitchen tap, the ubiquitous electricity that comes to our homes to give life to a host of devices, each a complex system of its own.

We Are Mechanisms

Three years ago, as I was charging down a city street on my mountain bike, a sixteen-year-old driver veered across my path. I slammed into the side of her SUV and was launched over its roof, landing on the pavement on the other side. To this day, I don't remember either of the impacts.

I was knocked unconscious, coming awake only as I was loaded into the ambulance. On the way to the hospital, the paramedic asked my name. I answered correctly. Then she asked who she could call to inform that I was going to the hospital. I told her "Linda." Then she asked me where I had been on my bike and . . . I just couldn't remember. It was several hours before I could put the pieces together, to recall the details of my ride.

From this experience, a lesson was hammered home: Our minds and bodies are complex *mechanisms*. They are machines that perform—or don't perform. They are indescribably complex collections of subsystems, operating via countless sequential and cooperative protocols. Our incredibly complex minds and bodies work well most of the time, but because of the occasional mechanical glitch within a subsystem, sometimes they don't.

We should never take for granted our connection to the reality around us; never underestimate the tenuous grip we have on our worlds. We must handle our bodies and minds with care; we should be careful about upkeep and maintenance, yet challenge them so they stay strong. We must attend to them and never take them for granted.

Contemplate the clothes we wear, the shopping we do, the work we perform. Consider the gas pumped into our cars at gas stations. In some faraway place, sophisticated mechanisms extract oil from the ground. Then people transport it via high-tech ships, trucks, and pipelines to refineries where the oil is converted into gasoline via complex refining processes. Next, truckers deliver the gasoline to an uncountable number of convenient locations so we can pump it into our cars whenever we feel like it. We never think twice about the intricacies of the drilling/refining/ delivery systems. And this is just one of the millions of systems that touch our daily lives.

And what about the human body? Consider the amazing complexity of chemicals, electric signals, and mechanics that make it work. For each of us, billions of cells contribute to who we are, while trillions of simultaneous electrical signals execute without overt supervision as we progress through the day. Incredible!

Consider the miracle of what you are doing this moment, viewing and translating the English language characters on this page. You are transferring my thoughts to your mind, where you instantaneously interact with what I am saying, making immediate judgments, agreeing or disagreeing, line by line.

Do these complex systems sometimes fail? Of course! Nonetheless, it's a numbers game, and it is unquestionable that the systems of our lives, taken together, work perfectly more than 99.9 percent of the time.

So far, I have focused on human systems, which are just a fraction of the total systems at work in any given second. Uncountable natural systems add to the numbers and dwarf what man has created, and they all work perfectly according to their scripts.

Once one accepts the world's beautiful "systems dance" for what it is, the mystery of it goes even deeper. Consider that primary systems depend on subsystems and those subsystems depend on sub-subsystems branching outward and downward, further and further, to subprimal levels.

And see that the processes of the world—the systems—repeat themselves over and over, as they incrementally create new forms and dissolve old ones.

Stop for a moment and attempt to draw it all in. The depth and intricacy of life's fabric is astonishing beyond comprehension. Try to grasp the beautiful complexity of life's workings and know that all by itself this world gurgles and percolates along with no overall human supervision. The countless systems that comprise life churn on and on while most of us remain oblivious to the perfection of it, to the mystery of it.

It's interesting that the two most opposite groups imaginable share the wonder of the world's miraculous workings: scientists and the religious.

I am neither promoting nor discounting the existence of a supreme being's controlling influence in maintaining this powerful, intriguing efficiency. The point here is that, for whatever reason, the wonderful flow of life carries on exquisitely, repeating and synchronizing over and over again, without some human's guidance. The sun comes up and later goes down. Grass grows in the spring and lies dormant in the winter. The tides rise and fall. We go to bed at night to wake up in the morning. The toaster works! The car works! Love comes, love goes, and then it comes again. We live, then we die, and another is born. Systems, systems, systems—everywhere!

A PROPENSITY FOR EFFICIENCY AND ORDER

I asked myself, could it be that the common presumption that says that the world is not functioning well—the world is a mess—is *wrong*? Yes, I realized, that presumption *is* wrong, because in any given life, on any given day, countless events and connections—systems—work perfectly. We don't notice them and so we take them for granted, never appreciating the impeccability of it all. We hyperfocus on personal, mechanical, and geopolitical systems that are not to our liking and conclude that deficiency is the default way of the world. Swallowed up in this, we see perfection as an anomaly and imperfection as the norm. That conclusion is backward.

Overall, the systems of this world work absurdly well: 99.9 percent of everything works just fine, and even the parts we consider imperfect are that way only because we think those parts should be different. (In truth, the world is 100 percent perfect if we discount what we want. However, for our purposes, let's *not* discount what we want. For practicality, let's characterize the world as 99.9 percent perfect.)

I lay in bed in wired stupor, thinking about how this world relentlessly churns ahead within a framework of countless efficient systems, and since there is no human King of Everything, that there has to be an underlying cosmologic propensity toward efficiency and order. Something out there prefers things to go smoothly.

God?

This new understanding was the reverse of my previous vision of things in which I saw the world as a place of barely controlled mayhem, tenuously held together by its human masters. I had visualized perfection—a rare thing—as an occasional harmonious chord in a universe more comfortable in its cacophony.

My mind continued to race that night in 1999, and it struck me that if the universe has a predilection for order, it should be a simple thing to "climb on board." Since system inefficiencies comprise such a small percentage of the things of my life, and because I have free will, I should be able to methodically isolate problematic systems and then, one by one, manipulate their mechanics to make them efficient. It should be easy because cosmological bias is on my side—and this bias is not just rooting for efficiency, it's demanding it!

THE POWER AND THE WHY

Is there a real-time analogy for the relentless power that propels the systems of the world? Yes. Find train tracks and stand nearby while a train slams by at full speed. Feel the overwhelming strength and inevitability of it. As the enormous mass of the train surges, feel the invincibility. This is an in-the-guts sense of the universe's mechanical potency and purposefulness. It's *that* deliberate.

The world's turning is powerful and systematic and that is the point. Why it behaves that way is the human mystery—the ultimate question—but it is not the issue at hand. What matters here is this: Despite the common assumption that chaos reigns, the truth is that the mechanics of the world work very, very well. And if we can proceed from the premise that there is a proclivity for powerful efficiency, rather than society's general assumption that all is chaos, we will stop fighting things. Instead, confident and deliberate, we can dig a bit deeper and, step-by-step, construct the lives we want.

GUMMING UP THE WORKS

Of course, it must be said that although there is a regulatory force disposed to keep systems flowing, human free will enables us to cause havoc on personal and global scales. When a system doesn't produce the outcome we want it to produce because of something we did or didn't do, we must recognize this is the downside of the human race's gift of being able to influence and control systems.

Dysfunctional systems may constitute just a small percentage of all systems, but for the record, let's state the obvious: We humans are inclined to disrupt things, and for this reason there have been and continue to be horrible problems in the world. The worst of it? In the last century, in fits of narcissistic insanity, tens of millions of people were slaughtered by Hitler, Mao, Stalin, Mussolini, and Pol Pot. These were human systems gone haywire. And still the agony continues, at its most virulent in third-world countries.

Then there is the self-generated personal pain of our own making, residing within our own thought processes. Add to this the self-inflicted damage caused by the neglect and abuse of the body systems that we inhabit, not to mention no-fault setbacks such as accidents and genetic irregularities: the *Forrest Gump* "sh*t happens" scenario (a brief yet profoundly meaningful phrase).

Large or small, cultural genocide or a missed appointment, the things that go wrong are due to component failures within systems. When a system fails to produce what we want it to produce, something within the system is not as it could be. Something is gumming up the works.

Despite all this, and notwithstanding the general media's allegations otherwise, the majority of lives move from beginning to end with a minimum of true, overt anguish. When there is trauma, it is most often short-lived. For most of us, real discomfort is a small slice of the pie, and when it happens, it is usually the result of self-inflicted mental anguish and fear—negative constructs within our thinking, not overt external, physical pain. Yes, again, of course there are the notable exceptions. I am not a Pollyanna.

Because the universe's overwhelming inclination is toward stability and efficiency, the events that go wrong in a typical person's life are but a small percentage of that person's total experience. *Systems want to be efficient.* If a system could talk, it would say, "My single goal—and I am passionate about it—is to accomplish the task that I was built to accomplish!" This means that our personal efforts to make things right are aided by an enigmatic power that works hard to propel those efforts to success. Within one's life, getting things to work swimmingly is not a difficult task if one pays attention to the mechanics of how things work.

Late that night, lying awake in bed, I realized the force *is* with you.

SAFETY, COMFORT, AND PC
IN THE FIRST AND THIRD WORLDS

Why are there major differences between life in the Western world and life in, say, Afghanistan or rural China? Why is life in the West easier than life in the East? A part of the answer is that, in the Western world, there are far more safety and protective systems than in the East, therefore our lives are less in jeopardy. A simple example: In the West, we wear seat belts in our cars 99 percent of the time. It's the law—and the law is a system. In the many times I have been to the rural Far East, I have seldom seen a driver or passenger buckle up. In most third-world countries, there are no enforceable seat belt laws. (Are seat belts actually in the cars? Yes, they usually lay buried in the seat cushions—but sometimes the driver has alto-gether removed them . . .)

Another example: Here in the West, there are quick and severe penal-ties for anyone's non-cause, assertive aggression toward another. In much of the East there are few protections, and justice systems can be corrupt and impotent, causing person-to-person and governmental crimes to go unpunished.

And the flip side? It is telling that the annoyance of the politically cor-rect is nowhere but in the West. This is a result of a culture trying too hard to regulate. It's system-thought taken to the extreme by people whose basic needs are satisfied and who have the time and energy to attempt to channel the thoughts and actions of others. To the rural Asian, there is no PC thinking, as life is negotiated via just a few systems, systems having to do with survival. In most of the world, people don't have the luxury of expending energy on politically correct gyrations.

For a Westerner, it is a good thing to live for a while in a third-world household. It's a crash course in fundamental priorities, personal humility, and root systems.

COMPONENT FAILURES AND SEMI-ENLIGHTENMENT

For me, one plus one equals two. For you, one plus one also equals two. The natural mechanics of the world are reliable and can be trusted. And human-devised systems will also operate reliably if they are put together properly and then maintained. If they are not put together correctly or they are not maintained, they will fail to produce the results we want.

Few people think their problems are a result of system failure. Most see their troubles as isolated events, blaming fate, horoscopes, bad luck, karma, God, the devil, neighbors, competitors, family members, the weather, the president, Congress, liberals, conservatives, global warming, too much TV, lack of money, too much money, the educational system, or just a world gone bad. And most see problems as overwhelming in num-ber: an onslaught from "out there," only to be fended off by superhuman efforts. For many, the excuse/blame list is endless. I had been a lifelong resident of that camp, but when the systems' vision engulfed me, there was zero chance I would ever live in that place again.

I now float through the day in fascination. Instead of wallowing in a hodgepodge of unpredictability and fire-killing, I see events and objects as part of one structured system or another. This real-time outside-and-slightly-elevated perspective has channeled peace and prosperity into my life and in the lives of those who depend on me. I call it semi-enlightenment.

Negatives will sometimes worm their way into my day, most often due to my own failures. It's not often, though—not any more.

This life I lead is a result of actions, actions rooted in my gut certainty that *in the systems that compose the world's workings, there is not a cosmic inclination for chaos. Rather, there is a default propensity toward order and efficiency.* Without question, I know inefficiency and its attending pain occur because of rare and isolated component problems within otherwise perfect systems.

THE HEART OF THE METHODOLOGY

By fixing your life's individual systems—by identifying them one at a time and then rebuilding them one by one—order, control, and peace accumulate incrementally. However, the improvements in these rebuilt systems must be made permanent or the systems will slip back into dysfunction due to random outside influence. In the workplace, permanence happens first by creating written descriptions of how systems are to operate, and second by making sure responsible parties follow the steps described in the documentation. We'll get to those details soon.

Once systems are examined and flawed components are exposed and repaired (tweaked), systems will produce the desired result. Creating new contributing systems and altogether eliminating dysfunctional systems will do the same. And since this is all mechanical, when the changes are performed and then locked in, improvement is both instant and permanent.

For your personal situation, not only can you count on an overwhelming bias toward efficiency but also you probably won't have a whole lot of systems to adjust, create, or delete. It won't take long to get things straightened out.

Now we are at the heart of the *Work the System* methodology. These lives we live are composed of countless linear systems, many of which are under our direct control. These systems are the invisible threads that hold the fabric of our lives together. If there is an outcome that doesn't suit us, we can change that outcome by making a component adjustment within a system, adding a system, or eliminating a system. In a life's rejuvenation, it will typically be "all of the above."

Whether an outcome is to your liking or not, the underlying system is performing exactly as it was constructed. You are not at the mercy of mysterious conspiring forces or of the swirling backwash of chaos. If it is in your power—and so much that affects you *is* in your power—you can fix things! What about those systems you can't repair because they are out of your control? Relax. If you can't fix something, don't worry about it. Do what you can, walk away, and accept it—or ignore it. But for sure, don't spend time or energy agonizing over it. If you live in a democracy, vote and then don't complain. If you have a problem with a coworker, talk to him or her and then don't obsess about the outcome. If you don't like the TV program, change the channel or turn off the set. Save your energy for efforts that will provide tangible positive results within your circle of influence.

THE OBJECTIVE

Back to my story, and the looming crisis at Centratel. That night in bed, yet another realization struck: My business needed at least one solid objective. From my new vantage point, I could see we had been operating without any pointed purpose. The closest I could come to a reason for the existence of the business was that I hoped we would "make money and be successful." That is the single mantra of the typical small-business owner or corporate middle manager. It is not concrete and directed but amorphous and wishy-washy.

Not only had I never considered its individual components, Centratel had no direction! Despite my jack-of-all-trades/fire-killer-extraordinaire comportment, I didn't have a grasp of the "why" of Centratel. To compound the confusion, there was no vision for my personal life either. This was the birth of the Strategic Objective document.

THE CRUX OF CONTROL:
THE SYSTEMS PERSPECTIVE

Without prodding, nor willing it to happen, I stepped outside my life, rose above it, and looked down, never again to settle back into the morass of my professional and personal lives. There was nothing philosophical about this new vantage point. It was mechanical and logical. I saw that the solution to my business problems did not lie in becoming more proficient at whacking mole heads—as in the Whac-A-Mole arcade and video games popular at that time—the solution was to find a way to eliminate the moles altogether. I had to put aside the hammer and dig down into those tunnels to find out exactly where the moles hid. When I found them, I would ruthlessly strangle them right then and there. Their grinning, furry faces would not distract me. And while I was down there taking care of mole extermination, I would find a way to prevent any mole relatives from returning later.

Late that night, my perspective on life permanently shifted. Deep in my gut, I grasped that perfectly executing systems were at play everywhere and all the time. My business—and my whole being, for that matter—was the sum total of the systems that composed it. Confident, I would look down on these systems of my life and isolate them one at a time, viewing each as a separate, autonomous entity. Per a solid directional plan, one by one, and over whatever period of time it would take, I would disassemble and then rebuild each system so that each contributed to my stated goal. In addition to the reconstruction, I would add new systems and discard useless ones.

It seemed logical: Creating efficient subsystems should cause the primary system to be efficient too. And to take this a step further, it seemed to me if the individual subsystems of my business and my life could be made more than efficient, if they were made potent and powerful, then both my business and my life would become potent and powerful. Who could argue with that logic? I just needed to identify individual subsystems and then, one by one, optimize them.

I hadn't been looking for a revelation, but in my desperation, I got one. It was a vision that bared the simple mechanics of the world, mechanics that had been cloaked by the dissonance of the day. It was a viewpoint that I would hone, and in the big picture and in the smallest snapshots of my life, I would no longer specialize in killing fires, spinning my wheels in futile attempts to stop chaos.

I would no longer manage the results of inefficient systems. Instead, I would expend my energies on perfecting those systems—and the results would take care of themselves.

For a decade and a half, although the simple reality had been floating right there in front of me, the mental turbulence of my fire-killing approach had relegated this simple earthshaking reality to invisibility: A life's condition is not the result of luck, or of being good or bad. And it's not about intelligence, karma, education, social class, political stance, religious affiliation, or how hard one works. Life is about simple mechanics— the dispassionate mechanics of the systems that compose it.

This new systems perspective was not just an interesting new concept; it was an electric, life-changing vision. Once the switch flipped in my head late that night, there was no going back. I was a changed man.

REBIRTH OF THE BUSINESS

It was uncanny. My thoughts raged on. Supported by indisputable logic, an entire strategy unfolded as I lay there that night.

I thought, if Centratel is an organism—like a human body, or a car, or a TV—smooth and efficient operation will depend on a multitude of simultaneously functioning systems that operate automatically.

In other words, the business systems I would fix and/or create would have to function without direct moment-to-moment supervision by me, the majority owner, general manager, and CEO of the company. To be sure, people would be watching things, but I would not be one of those people. The "watchers" would be system-improvement managers who would supervise the systems of the business without my constant over-the-shoulder intrusion. Centratel would become a self-perpetuating organism.

Further, this organism would be the highest-quality telephone answering service in the United States. We would accomplish this in three steps.

1. We would exactly define the overall goals and strategies. It would be done on paper by creating the Strategic Objective, and the General Operating Principles.

2. We would break down Centratel's workings into subsystems we could understand: processing calls, staff management, client services, equipment, quality control, the methodology for handling client and customer calls, bookkeeping, purchasing, customer services, etc. Then, each of those subsystems would be broken down into even smaller contributing sub-subsystems, including receivables software, customer complaint protocol, employee recruitment, equipment maintenance schedules, and so on.

3. Once isolated and exposed, we would refine and perfect those systems—one by one—so each would contribute 100 percent toward overall goals and each would automatically execute every time. As needed, we would create new systems from scratch and we would discard systems that didn't contribute. We would document each system by creating a Working Procedure for it, thus making all the perfected systems permanent. Through all of this we would be patient as we improved things incrementally.

FROM ORGANIC TO MECHANICAL

Why does a car perform the same way every time? Why does a city stay in the same place without spontaneously moving to a new location? Why do we, in our lifetimes, continue to be ourselves? The reason is hard mechanical reality: physicality. With the obvious exceptions of fluids and gases, physical objects don't morph into other physical objects or dissipate into the ether. They are dependable and predictable.

On the other hand, human communication processes—organic processes—are the antithesis of physical substance. The execution of a given recurring communication protocol not only varies among the individuals performing the process but also, for any one person, with the time of day, the weather, or mood. Uncontrolled, these organic processes are feathers in the wind.

In the workplace, the challenge and the solution is to make these ubiquitous organic human processes as solid and reliable as the mechanical objects that surround us. We do this with documentation.

STRENGTH AND RESILIENCE

In the process of rebuilding Centratel system by system, strength and resilience would evolve as by-products. The outside world would continue to challenge us with unexpected shake-ups, but if we constructed the new systems properly, the business would become rugged and adaptable. The inevitable earthquakes would be reduced to tremors. Until this point, earthquakes had been earthquakes, and there had been too many of them.

> If what I saw for the business was true—that it was a primary system composed of component subsystems, each of which could be brought to high efficiency and strength—then it was logical this would be true for the other primary system that was in immediate crisis: my physical and mental self.

The theory and process for fixing myself would be the same as it would be for fixing Centratel. That's the beauty of the *Work the System* method: It applies to any life situation because it deals with fundamental cause and effect—the basic truth of how the world mechanically operates.

Learning How to Sleep

For any recurring problem, there is a path to sorting things out: Take the inefficient system apart and fix the pieces one by one. Earlier I discussed my problems with getting enough sleep. Sleep intertwines with numerous other biological, social, and relationship processes, but in that broad conception, one can't begin to find a solution to improving it. What did I do via systems methodology to cure this problem? I envisioned sleep as an independent, primary system that is composed of subsystems.

The vision led me to a doctor who specializes in sleep disorders. The doctor's recommendations had a strong theme: reduction of stress. This led me to the subsystems of yoga, more sensible exercise, and meditation. I would substantially reduce my intake of caffeine, alcohol, and sugar. There were other systems to modify: changing the layout of my bedroom, removing the clock from the nightstand, refraining from reading in bed, and turning the lights off at the same time every night. I would adopt a more consistent system routine for preparing for sleep. Another thing: Testing indicated my requirements for sleep were less than average—six hours was enough—and so I should avoid lying awake in bed, expecting to get eight or nine hours. Lying there waiting for sleep to arrive was stressful in itself. Instead, I should get up and read, work, or even exercise.

With the help of my regular doctor, I found my blood chemicals were out of balance. Those chemical imbalances affected my sleep pattern, and it was a simple matter to fix those subsystem imbalances with supplements.

I had to reduce my hours at the office and that meant getting the company to run itself without me being there every minute. Of course, that transformation was already underway, using the same *Work the System* thinking.

I got back to a healthy sleeping routine over the course of just a few months, literally doubling each night's sleep duration.

Now, if I find that my sleep is less than what it should be, I can trace the problem back to a violation of one of the dozen or so system guidelines I initially identified in my "sleep system–improvement" project.

I attacked the overall problem by isolating the primary sleep system and then breaking it down into subsystems that could be manipulated. By taking an outside-and-slightly-elevated vantage point, I was able to tweak my sleep process to more and more efficiency, one piece at a time. It was pure mechanics.

Is there a major problem you are coping with right now? Can you break it down into segments? Can you modify the segments one at a time?

CHAPTER 5

Execution and Transformation

*Action is a great restorer and builder of confidence. Inaction
is not only the result, but the cause, of fear. Perhaps the
action you take will be successful; perhaps different action or
adjustments will have to follow. But any action is better than
no action at all.*

—Norman Vincent Peale

Until I woke up, my vision of the business was one of a mass of interrelated and confused events. Because of this presumption of chaotic complexity, unraveling was impossible. Observing the workings of Centratel
in a "holistic" way, I could not detect nor isolate the internal inefficiencies
that kept pecking away at things.

On a subliminal level, the feel-good precept that "everything is
related to everything else so we should consider each of our actions in a
global way" encourages paralysis while it masks problems. Any possibility
of internal improvement is subverted by the assumption that tampering
with things over here will upset things over there. The notion that a butterfly flapping its wings over the jungles of Brazil has an impact on the
weather patterns over New Hampshire is an interesting concept, but in
the real world it evokes a nonsensical and subtle paranoia. Although the
concept illustrates the interrelation of things, taking it literally casts a spell
of impotence over an individual's inclination to make changes. In the real
world of day-to-day existence, the Brazilian butterfly doesn't make a damn
bit of difference.

Now I understand that the reason I had felt helpless to fix my business and my personal life was because I had seen them as impenetrable entities. I never contemplated the notion of a process that would dissect them into simple subsystems that I could optimize one at a time. Instead of fixing the faulty mechanisms, I had been caught up in attending to the recurring problems those hidden faulty mechanisms had produced.

So the years had crawled by as I whacked the moles. It seemed there was no other option but to wallow in the middle of it and hope for some kind of magical, holistic solution: a huge loan from the bank, the perfect employee, client, or management consultant.

I could have spent my whole life like that!

But now I had the solution. I would disassemble Centratel, fix the pieces one by one, and put them back together again. If I did that, it seemed sensible that the finished product would be superior.

A NEW WORLD

My insights arrived just days prior to the payroll I was going to miss. We had to find the money to pay staff and keep them working so the repair process could begin. With newfound emotional energy, I convinced my credit card company to raise my credit limit a bit so some cash could be drawn. A friend gave me a loan. Offering a discount, I talked a client into paying for a year of answering service in advance. Several staff members agreed to delay cashing their paychecks.

We made it through the payroll crisis, and I immediately began to turn my attention to creating three sets of documents that would get Centratel on track: First, I would create the Strategic Objective, which would define us and set goals. Second, I would put together the General Operating Principles, which would serve as our guidelines for making decisions. Third, I would write out our Working Procedures, which would exactly define every recurring process of the business.

I created our Strategic Objective and began our Principles document. Then I explained this new vision to my staff, outlining what we would do next and how they were going to assume new management postures. Tentatively at first, we began creating our Working Procedures: isolating, fixing, and documenting systems one at a time. For examination and repair, we first selected the most flawed system and then moved on to the next most flawed. From the moment of my late-night epiphany, we were on a new path of system improvement and there was no turning back.

Marching ahead without pause, we quickly began to see results as confusion diminished and cash flow came under control. In the first six months, my workweek dropped from a hundred hours to sixty. Then, in the next six months, it fell below forty.

Much of our early success had to do with the perfection of our internal communication system. Every moment, each of us knew what was going on in other parts of the business, and each of us could make decisions without stumbling in semantics or bureaucracy. (You'll read more on communication in part three.)

We made all critical systems, both human and mechanical, redundant. The first year passed and we confidently hammered on. Customer and staff complaints steadily declined, and chaos dissolved into serenity as we relentlessly performed the work of improving systems.

Precisely targeting our efforts through our Strategic Objective and Principles documents, and then following up with Working Procedures, we tackled the obvious recurring protocols, gobbling up inefficiencies. Everything we did met the criteria of the new systems thinking. We perfected bookkeeping, operations, HR, vendor relations, customer service, quality control, and marketing. Forging ahead relentlessly, we rebuilt and documented several hundred existing systems, one by one. At the same time, we created new systems from scratch and discarded useless ones. Whew!

Through it all, there was some employee turnover. A couple of staff members wouldn't accept the new systems theory and attending documentation. They were replaced by fresh faces who bought into the systems game plan. (Today, we attract and keep smart, loyal, goal-oriented people because of *how* we operate. Also, because of our strict systemized approach, we are expert at sizing up people in job interviews. Of course, another reason for our great staff is because our compensation/benefit package is much higher than other businesses in our region, as well as the TAS industry at large. The high wages we pay are a result of the higher service rates we are able to charge, as well as the superefficient operation itself.)

As error rates plunged, the overall quality of our answering service dramatically improved, light years better than industry standards. The growth of the business went into high gear; within two years of instituting our new paradigm, we bought out all three of our local answering service competitors (and we bought five nonlocal ones as well). We absorbed both of our voice mail service competitors, too. In that two-year period, our TAS client base grew from three hundred to seven hundred.

It was system improvement at its finest, and to this day, we still spend most of our time "working our systems." The large-scale, overt repair work is finished, however, and today the system-improvement work only has to do with staying current with technological advances and market permutations.

In reflecting on those years of rebuilding, it took a long time to straighten things out. But as I look back, that's understandable because we were figuring out the details of the *Work the System* methodology from scratch. We invested (and sometimes inadvertently wasted) time and money as we experimented with new concepts, tried to find the right management people, and stumbled with the system documentation.

Our relationship with a third minor partner, for example, had an enormous negative impact. That partnership began in the middle of the rejuvenation and included sending some of our call processing chores overseas, which ultimately resulted in a severe loss of clients. This, in turn, led to full-blown legalities. In the end, we were able to buy the partners out of the company based upon a settlement agreement. But it's my guess that the bad partnership and resulting litigation cost us between two and three years of progress.

There was a lot to do because in addition to the rebuilding efforts and the litigation, we had a business to run. But, obviously, there was enough energy to do what we had to do. It was a long five years, but I recall them with nostalgia and satisfaction.

As mentioned, despite the setbacks and the additional workload, my physical involvement with the company's daily operations continued to decline. Today, I spend just a couple of hours a week working on Centratel business. One of those hours is for our weekly staff meeting and the other is for paying bills or attending to various R&D efforts.

If we were to do this again without having to develop the process from scratch, it would take fewer than eighteen months to reach the lifestyle and income we now enjoy.

HEART AND MIND

In parallel with the business resuscitation, there was no time to delay in regaining my personal health. As with the business, I had to change course right away, and it was obvious what I must do. I would handle my physical problems with the same systems methodology.

1. **I changed my viewpoint.** What, exactly, was making me ill? My doctor thought I was "depressed," and after gyrating around that theory for way too long, it suddenly became clear to me this was not the problem. In fact, my problems stemmed from undergoing too much external stress. I got outside and up, looked down, and saw my body as a collection of subsystems, many of which could be manipulated. My physical being was not a jumble of random happenings to which I could only react; it was a system of systems, and some of those systems were not performing adequately. As previously mentioned, I modified or eliminated certain stress-inducing systems in order to prevent stress events from occurring in the first place. (The biggest relief was in cutting back my office hours through the systemizing of Centratel.) Finally, to stop creating stress internally, I took the cognitive approach to eliminate negative thoughts as they emerged spontaneously.

2. **I created a personal written plan.** I wrote a simple one-page controlling document in which I described my goals and guidelines—a personal Strategic Objective. I also created a personal

Operating Principles document that included a series of "stress-reducing action items."

3. **Once things got better, I continued to perform stress-reducing action items on a regular basis.** Always working toward the ideal, but not always reaching it, this preventative maintenance is what I have to do to stay healthy. That's it! The mantra of the *Work the System* method is to isolate-fix-maintain. *It is not enough to know what to do. One must take action.* What good is knowledge unless something changes for the better because of it?

Stress-Reducing Action Items

It started with a simple list. I wrote down five or six actions that would reduce stress. I carried the note in my pocket for a few days, jotting down additional ideas as they came to mind. My final list included fifteen "action items," each a separate system of its own. These items were not special in any way; most people would agree that any one of them would help eliminate stress.

Here's the original raw list: work fewer hours, lose ten pounds, go to the sleep disorder clinic to find out how to sleep, stop ingesting caffeinated drinks, learn meditation and yoga.

Exercise vigorously but not excessively at least four times a week. Eat good food. Drink lots of water. Ingest less sugar and salt. Get a blood test every three months and per those tests, take supplements until my chemicals come into balance. See friends at least once a week. Spend more one-on-one time with my family. Read a minimum of one hour each day: one book and half a dozen periodicals per week.

While I compiled the list, my thought was that it would be sensible to choose just some of the items on the list, whichever ones seemed best. However, when the list was complete, I decided to implement all fifteen items, leaving nothing out. Why should any of them be dismissed if each one contributed to my well-being? It was a tough, challenging list, difficult to fully implement, but I gave it my best shot. I viewed each of my action items as separate subsystems and incorporated them into the overall system that is my life. Because I had been such a mess, it took two years to get healthy again. Fifty years of stress damage was not unraveled overnight.

Today, do I live every minute by these standards? No, but I get close.

 ## Paying the Bills

Here is an example of replacing an old system with a new one.

For years, a nagging problem at Centratel was the time and effort it took to pay the monthly bills. The process did nothing for the bottom line, and each month required ten to fourteen hours of my time to process sixty to eighty payables to various vendors. I wrote the checks, entered the transactions into the check register, stuffed the checks into envelopes, and mailed them. Then there was the filing and bookkeeping. As we grew, it became too time-consuming for me, so I hired a part-time bookkeeper. But that created another problem because the expenditures were not being questioned by our bookkeeper in the painstaking way I would question them.

The system solution: Our bank's online "Billpayer" feature. This system is a perfect illustration of *Work the System* thinking and methodology. Now, writing a hard-copy check seldom happens. Ninety percent of recurring monthly bills are the same amount each month, so the system is programmed to pay these bills automatically. QuickBooks automatically logs these monthly payments, too. For a payable in which the billed amount changes monthly, it's an easy matter for me to review the invoice and then insert the amounts both online and in QuickBooks.

Now, again paying the bills personally, I am able to keep a close eye on every cent of expenditure.

This is a prime example of investing time to set up a new system and then benefiting forever from the effort. Over several weeks, it took fifteen hours to work out the bugs and program our vendors into the system—the same amount of time that had been required each month to pay bills with the old system. Now I spend maybe two or three hours a month to process these payables.

At home? It's the same process. The homeowner association dues, water, electricity, and everything else are paid on time with very little input from me.

Are we outside and slightly elevated? Yes! Billpayer is the quintessential illustration of systems methodology, an enormous success for us at work and at home. I will be bold here: If you are not using it now, you should be.

How many bills do you have that occur every month? How do you pay them? If you pay by check and mail, ask yourself how much time it takes each month and then multiply that by twenty years. How much total time is that? And how much does it cost in checks, envelopes, and postage? Would it be worthwhile to spend several hours to set up a simple bill-payer system and cut the bill-paying time by 90 percent?

CHAPTER 6

Systems Revealed, Systems Managed

*A person needs new experiences. They jar something deep
inside, allowing him to grow. Without change, something sleeps
inside us, and seldom awakens. The sleeper must awake!*

— Duke Leto Atreides (Jürgen Prochnow)
from the movie *Dune* (Universal, 1984)

Note to the reader: *This chapter and the next have a meditative quality.
You must ingrain the* Work the System *method, so in an attempt to get you
there, I present these two chapters in a repetitive, almost hypnotic tone. I thoroughly describe the core of the mind-set while adding some new elements.*

CONVERGING CHAINS

Your day can be calm, predictable, and under control. Chronic shortages of
time and money, gun-to-the-head decision making, and dealing with less-
than-amusing people can be history. Order and calm can replace anxiety.
Starting with a subtle shift of perspective, elimination of chaos is possible.

This is about a simple mind-set change that will cause subsequent
modification in how you handle the subsystems that make up the system-
of-systems that is you. The pathway to control—to eliminating chaos—is
to discover, examine, optimize, and then manage your mechanical and
biological systems. The dictionary's definition of *system* is "a group of
interacting, interrelated, or interdependent elements forming a complex
whole." That's perfect.

In every aspect of your being, systems are wall-to-wall. In linear 1-2-3 sequences, they are embedded everywhere, operating all the time. You wake, study, read, exercise, and eat. You breathe, walk, and digest. You go to work, talk to friends, drive to the store to pick up groceries for dinner. You put gas in the car. You earn money and put it in the bank; later, you pay the bills.

Silent and invisible, your systems work without pause. Sometimes they work alone, but often they work together. They support and complement each other—and sometimes they fight each other.

These processes—these systems—are most often recurring, not one-time events. And you can make improvements in many of your systems, manhandling them into efficiency, pointing them in the directions you want them to point, producing the results you want them to produce.

As you examine the systems of your life, investigating your way down through the multiplying, expanding, and intertwining rootlike chains, you see that subsystems compose each system, and each subsystem is composed of sub-subsystems. Turn things around and work your way back up to the top of the converging chains. As they come together and thicken into a single trunk, see that they add up to the primary system that is you. You are a system of systems!

The essence of your work, health, and relationships lies within systems, and although veiled behind the buzz of everyday consciousness, there is nothing magical or esoteric about them—or about their management. You will see life for what it is, a collection of individual linear systems; then, in this clarity, you will extract and perfect these systems one by one before reinserting each back into your life. The huge and wonderful irony of these machinations is that peace and prosperity silently enter through the side door.

NEARING YOUR EPIPHANY

Grasp that each of the countless systems of your world is linear, a process. Like computer program code, they execute their steps in sequence. I'll say it again: More often than not, the systems are recurring; they happen over and over again.

This is important, and notwithstanding a physicist's space/time theoretical objections, a system doesn't execute randomly. It operates in a simple, predictable, 1-2-3, step-by-step progression. Ruthless and relentless, it proceeds the same way every single time unless a component is adjusted, removed, or inserted.

Right now, slow things down for yourself. Find a place where you won't be distracted. Visualize each of the following systems, focusing on their 1-2-3-step sequences.

- Start with the closed set of sequential actions for driving a car from point A to point B. (Open the car door, get in, put the seat belt on, insert the key in the ignition, turn the key to start the engine, etc.)

- Describe the specific linear steps—both mechanical and human— involved in finding a potential customer, making a presentation, and closing a sale. Consider the process of interviewing and hiring a new employee and then keeping this person for the long term while maximizing his or her contribution. Think about nurturing a relationship with a spouse, coping with terminal illness, or giving birth. Then there are the mundane processes of preparing a financial report, writing a paper for a college course, raking the yard, or doing the wash.

- Go back to the miraculous human-body system that propels you through this world with its countless individual biological and mechanical subsystems, nearly all of which function without any overt guidance, but many of which are under your control to enhance or to abuse.

Use your imagination and see uncountable system sequences in motion, most going unnoticed—unless there is this deliberate observation. You see that some sequences don't matter too much, but others have an enormous effect on your happiness and the happiness of those around you.

Yes, systems and subsystems intertwine and affect each other, yet first they are separate entities. Although most all of your life-systems are automatic, there are many you perform consciously. Focusing on these systems that are under your conscious direction, you'll see that tweaking each to higher efficiency is nearly always possible. You can add brand-new systems, too. Others you'll discard.

The *Work the System* methodology itself is a system. It's the controlling management tool used to analyze and maintain your personal systems. It's the master control mechanism for organizing yourself into an efficient life: a life of serenity, prosperity, and contribution.

SYSTEM MANAGEMENT

Each of your personal systems has direction and thrust. Each is headed somewhere, attempting to accomplish something. Systems and subsystems are channeled by genetically determined patterns, learned formulas, cultural codes, bias based on race and gender, humanitarian predilections, simple self-interest, and of course the standard physical predispositions for appetite, sleep, sex, and survival. And all of them are propelled by a mysterious force that many of us choose to call God.

So each of us is a system of systems. But here's the rub: Some of our personal systems—each of which, always remember, can be visualized as a distinct entity—are headed in oblique directions, confusing our efforts to reach our conscious goals. At best, a system combines efforts with other systems to help us reach desired targets. At worst, an errant component within a system creates problems that manifest themselves chaotically, chronically, and often subversively, contributing to the feeling that one is not in proper control of one's life. That out-of-control feeling is not rare:

Many people are *not* in control of their lives, especially if the definition of control includes the qualifier "I am getting what I want in my life."

The system-of-systems view of things sounds complicated, but the complexity of life doesn't leave you helpless to gain control of things because, one at a time, you can take action on specific system components that you draw out of the complexity. This is management in its most elemental form, and the beautiful thing is that neither the sheer complexity of it all, nor your propensity to lean in certain directions, will stop you from improving the mechanical/human systems that turn the wheels of your life.

You can list a multitude of individual systems that are necessary for just getting through the day, not to mention running a business, holding a job, coping with college, raising children, making retirement vibrant and meaningful—or just staying levelheaded while balancing a household, negotiating with family members, and providing an income. (I was a single parent for fifteen years and—don't argue with me—this role is the supreme test of a human's ability to simultaneously kill fires, build something for the future, and stay sane.)

In our culture it is common to call the management of the day's myriad events "multitasking" or "polyphasic activity." These are flawed expressions because they suggest the performance of multiple simultaneous tasks is some kind of laudable accomplishment.

Per the *Work the System* method, the term "system management" is what we're after, the term to replace multitasking. System management describes a thought-out orchestration, a demonstration of moment-to-moment control in which one has a firm grip on details and is not living at the edge of crisis, floating along on hope, fingers crossed, prayers recited, and obsessions indulged.

The focus must be on the proactive management of systems, not on coping with random system results.

If the majority of time is spent examining and tweaking systems to perfection, great results will materialize. Conversely, think about "holistic" solutions that cover life's complexity like a blanket: Another market for the product, a better manager for the company, a larger house, a new boss, a new spouse. These are attempts to straighten things out all at once and, although obviously applicable in some situations, are opposite of the continuous efforts I am proposing here.

Stop looking for a sudden hand-of-God solution to problems. Drop the idea that life is convoluted and mysterious, strip away the complexity, and get to work repairing the underlying inefficient mechanisms one by one. Trying to find peace and personal control through drugs, food, work, money, esoteric psychobabble, fanatical adherence to religious or political dogma, running away, or excessive preoccupation with the external— obsession—is an abomination of the simplicity of it all. These blanket applications falsely promise to soothe life's complexities in one fell swoop. Instead, the *Work the System* methodology goes inside and fixes building-block components one at a time. It's about making small, mechanical system improvements rather than being swallowed up by the promise of some cure-all that only masks chronic internal inefficiency.

Let's set aside the complexity and find a way to manage the mechanics of the systems that are right in front of us. The first steps you'll take include setting direction and deciding on strategy. (You will begin this process by creating the Strategic Objective and the General Operating Principles. These documents are fully explained in chapter 10.)

THE SUBVERSIVE HOLISTIC THOUGHT PROCESS

According to the *American Heritage Dictionary*, there are two definitions of *holistic*. First, "emphasizing the importance of the whole and the interdependence of its parts." Second, "concerned with wholes rather than analysis or separation into parts." Clearly, the *Work the System* methodology is the antithesis of the second definition. Yet the *results* of the methodology are in exact accordance with the first definition. In the last thirty years, the terms *holistic* and *global* have inserted themselves into the fabric of our culture, supposing "if we do this over here, it will have consequences over there, so let's not do anything" or "the entire system is faulty, so let's entirely replace it," etc. These generalizations create a paralysis in which we don't take any action at all, or we identify a problematic primary system, assume the entire primary system is faulty, and then try to force an overall replacement—without first examining the subsystem components.

Too often we go after a holistic, bumper-sticker solution when it would be more sensible to simply examine the primary system's context and fix a faulty component. From the start, the overall primary system is probably better than okay, working well in most situations. Could we apply a minor internal adjustment to bring things closer to perfection instead of disrupting or replacing the entire system?

SYSTEM IMPROVEMENT AND WORKING PROCEDURES

If you are like most people, you do not consciously consider the involvement of systems in your daily life. Therefore, you have not consciously thought in terms of adjusting systems in order to eliminate problems from occurring in the first place. For most people, whacking emerging moles is the only option considered. There is no thought of burrowing deep into the mole hole for some serious mole extermination.

The little moles are cute-faced decoys that distract us from the critical moves we should be making. I say, let's burrow deep inside their tunnels and eradicate them all. And then, before we leave, let's do some system adjusting—let's do what we have to do—so no more moles show up later. Then, confident that moles will never distract us again, we'll climb back above ground and start fixing the other systems of our lives that need fixing.

Here is a mechanical truth of how the world works: One can compensate for the negative outcome of a recurring problem, but without repairing the errant system that caused the problem, the problem will undoubtedly occur again.

Few people understand the systems-management approach of successful managers who intuitively grasp that a seemingly isolated problem is not isolated at all. These leaders see problems as the result of a flaw in an errant system—an errant system they can fix. For these pacesetters (more often from the corporate world than from government), a problem is not a disappointment just to be corrected and then written off. It's a wake-up call. This means that once the manager corrects the immediate negative effects, there is a second step. It is this second step that is key: The problem's cause is traced to the errant subsystem, which is then modified so that the problem doesn't happen again.

Through the astute leader's observation, a problem calls for a subsystem modification. The leader makes the permanent improvement, causing the entire system to be incrementally more robust and reliable than before the problem occurred. Addressing the problem, and then taking this second step to fix the cause of the problem, distinguishes the people who are in control from the people who are not in control—the successful from the unsuccessful.

So the improvement of a system is a system improvement, and the documentation of that system improvement is called a Working Procedure. The documentation of each improved system is critical. Making a system improvement without it guarantees that the improved system will revert to an inefficient unpredictability borne of shortcuts, outdated but comfortable methodologies, the pressures of the day, and/or confusion infused by assorted personalities and talents. Documentation gives permanence to your system improvements. It has to happen.

Again, by focusing on repairing problems in this way, the primary system becomes ever more efficient. Over time, rough edges dissolve.

It's a beautiful thing, this system-improvement process, because as time passes things improve. *Imagine a system that improves with time rather than wears out.*

At the start, these one-by-one system improvements can seem daunting. You work at them for a while and then ask, "When will the problems cease, and when can I stop fixing and documenting things?" But you carry on despite the demanding work ahead. After plugging along for a while, you notice the pace and quantity of incoming problems decrease. You see the fire-killings aren't coming so fast, and this is the point where a powerful belief takes hold. With fervor, you accelerate the system-improvement/ working-procedure process so even fewer errors occur, and your organization and personal life become smooth and efficient. The bottom line improves while personal vitality increases. Things come under control! You'll never go back.

Permanence

As the *Work the System* methodology is applied, your focus is on fixing one system after another, not careening through the day randomly taking care of whatever problems erupt. Your job is not to be a fire-killer. Your job is to prevent fires. Of course, in daily life you will always encounter fire-killing, but the idea is to minimize it.

RIPPLES AND HEAVY SEAS

For Centratel, the system-improvement process continues nine years after the implementation of the *Work the System* method. Now, problems are so few that when one surfaces, my staff pounce on it with a vengeance. It is hard to describe the satisfaction of leading a company that operates this way. Like the business, my personal life still has its occasional unexpected ups and downs (that's life!), but now it is enormously more resilient and I am well prepared to absorb unexpected blows. For the apple vendor, an overturned apple cart is a disaster, but an apple falling off the side of the cart now and then is a small, easily managed occurrence. There is no getting away from making mistakes and from random problems that are caused by an unexpected circumstance or a simple unpredictable human error.

The good news is that in organizations and in personal lives, outright mistakes and random errors account for only a small percentage of total errors. Most problems stem from nonexistent system management and show themselves as errors of omission. The further good news is that the *Work the System* method dramatically reduces this form of inefficiency. (Errors of omission are addressed in part three.)

What about the unexpected heavy seas of a debilitating injury or the loss of a loved one? Here it is again: Strength and resilience are by-products of the *Work the System* method. A life that is stronger and more resilient will be better able to navigate the inevitable dark waters.

TWEAKING

Once the one-time repair of errant systems is complete, the system manager focuses on routine reviews of the entire collection of systems. Per the *Work the System* method, an important aspect of everyday life is to examine established systems on a regular basis and to make system improvements as required. This ongoing review process keeps life smooth over the long term.

With the *Work the System* method, the percentage of time and effort expended fixing systems decreases with time, while the percentage of time and effort expended on improving systems, what I call "tweaking," increases with time. Since much of the recaptured time and energy is reinvested in refining more subsystems, the primary system becomes ever more efficient and powerful. This is the "cycle of increasing returns."

NOTICING POOR SYSTEM MANAGEMENT

When you get a feel for system management in your daily life, you will notice when it isn't happening around you. As you interact with the world, you'll find yourself critiquing what works and what doesn't, aware of not only your personal systems and their quality of execution but also of the systems others manage. This new posture as an informal "service quality observer" will go with you everywhere.

Once you get the systems perspective, you will see fire-killing all around you.

You will understand the real reasons why people who promise to call don't call; why there is lousy service in certain restaurants, retail stores, and hotels; why there is haphazard communication with a service provider. You will develop a knack for instantly recognizing shoddy workmanship, missed deadlines, promises not kept, bad attitudes, and sloppy execution. These dysfunctional human performances are the logical end result of poor system management, both organizational and personal. Human dysfunction is pervasive. You can't miss it. The better you get at system management, the more you will notice these inefficiencies. But when you encounter efficiency and calm in a business, an organization, or another individual, you will notice that, too, and you will recognize it as the beautiful thing it is.

What is the most important difference between the manager of a large successful business and the manager of a small struggling business? The first manages systems; the second copes with bad results.

When you're at the receiving end of poor service, remember that the ultimate problem is not with the person who is facing you, who may indeed be rude or uncaring, but with the individual at the top of the organization who is not managing properly. Even so, be sympathetic with the absent leader. Most people don't understand the system-improvement process, or even that there is such a thing. With best intentions, and working hard, they muddle along, batting off the fastballs as they come hurtling in from all directions. I was like that.

What about selfish people? Yes, some are ready to circumvent the rules as they ignore common expectations and don't consider others. But be careful here, too. Don't confuse someone's personality flaw with their mechanical problem, which is a simple lack of attention to the details of personal relationship systems. How one goes about cultivating good relationships is also a system, and the methodology must be set up with care and executed with consistency. For thoughtless people, the base problem is not a personality flaw but the lack of a functional "relationship maintenance system." This is a vicious circle. These people do not return calls, remember birthdays, send thank-you notes, or extend invitations. They don't show the least interest in the vicissitudes of the people around them. The consequence is that they receive little positive attention in return. These lonely people feel rejected and alienated and they reflect that rejection and alienation, digging themselves deeper and deeper into loneliness. Is it their fault? Well, yes it is.

But it's not about a "bad" person. It's about the absence of system management. It sounds antiseptic but it's the reality: Some people don't apply the system fundamentals necessary to make and keep friends. Maybe they don't care enough, or more probably, they just don't get it.

Despite the near perfection of our mechanical world, look around you right now and notice that the human qualities of dependability and consistency are in short supply. And because they are in short supply, people accept that condition as normal; actually, people should accept it as normal. It *is* normal, and happily for you, that means standing out from the crowd won't take much effort.

Once *Work the System* protocols are functional in your life, the people around you will start to notice your quick execution of detail, your consistent reliability, and the congruency between what you say and what you do, and especially, your calm, confident comportment. New customers, great employees, and reliable friends will be attracted to you because you doggedly adhere to the simple system-management tenets for cultivating great personal and business relationships. People can depend on you.

YOUR LIFE: PROBLEMATIC OR ORDERLY?

So, bottom line, how do you perceive your life? Do you see it as problematic—unfair, unpredictable, and inhospitable? Or do you view it as orderly and in control, ready to do your bidding?

Yet again, this isn't a matter of having a positive or a negative attitude or adopting some philosophical stance based on esoteric theory. This is about simplicity, mechanics, and logic.

How do you see things?

A Certain Billionaire

We were on vacation in Siena, Italy. We'd been there just a few days and at night the jet lag had me either entertaining strange dreams or lying awake. This particular night, it was both. An interesting midnight dream inspired this 2:00 a.m. writing session.

In the vivid dream, a well-known multibillionaire asked me to take the equivalent of the chief operations officer position for his conglomeration of international corporations.

Upon receiving the offer in this tycoon's ad hoc boardroom located on the tarmac of an airport somewhere, my central dream-thought as I faced him was I would succeed. I would succeed despite my small-town heritage, my lack of an advanced educational degree, and the shortage of other seemingly necessary background requisites. My challenges would be prosaic, limited to dealing with frequent travel, the certain inevitable corporate personality clashes, and whether or not being a part of the enterprise would cause me to feel trapped in a cage (my current world is much smaller, but at least I call the shots).

In my dream, why was I confident? It was because my position would entail dealing with the same simple mechanical realities of cause and effect that I deal with now, just on a larger scale. I would work my systems in this enormous corporate structure where, metaphorically speaking, one plus one would continue to equal two, just like everywhere else. Other than the scale of the endeavor, my tasks would be no different from the tasks I accomplish now.

Do you think you would be confident if you had a similar dream? Why or why not? Can you "scale-up" your present work into something with a larger impact? From a strictly mechanical standpoint, what is the next logical level of advancement in a key part of your life?

CHAPTER 7

Getting It

I'm trying to free your mind but I can only show you the door.
You're the one who has to walk through it.

—MORPHEUS (LAURENCE FISHBURNE)
FROM THE MOVIE *THE MATRIX* (WARNER BROS., 1999)

IMAGINE THIS SCENARIO. Recently it became clear that one of the managers in the company where you work had neglected his department, and it showed in the lack of output, the number of problems, and the general chaos.

You feel bad the department manager lost his job, but you understand why it happened. You are a troubleshooter for your organization, and your assignment is to straighten things out. You make your way to the department, which occupies a single room in your building.

You walk through a door into a large, well-lit room, one that you have been in many times before. Surrounding you are dozens of wooden boxes varying in size from one to four feet square. The closed, unlocked boxes, each with a hinged wooden lid, are scattered around the room. You begin by pushing the boxes around so they are in order, taking the time to organize them so you can work in a logical, efficient way.

You've brought your toolbox, and of course, you have written technical instructions should there be questions. The repair and maintenance procedures are understandable and well thought-out.

Because of the previous neglect of the contents of these boxes, you knew before you came here that completing this job would require a long day. You hunker down and get to work.

You open the lid of the first box and find inside a single system, a mechanical apparatus. It's made up of gears, wires, and levers, and because you are a technician trained in understanding the construction of such devices, what you see makes sense. It's a simple thing, really. It is clear to you what this device does and how it is put together. Peering into the box, examining the system, it is apparent that mechanical adjustments are necessary. You make the adjustments. In the course of your work, you notice an obsolete component. You replace it with an updated version (you always carry spares). This upgrade will make the device more efficient and reliable.

Then, you oil all the moving parts and finish by cleaning up the mechanism, wiping it off. You test the system to make sure it's working perfectly. It is.

On the inside of the lid you write the date and your initials, along with a brief summary of what you did so that when someone else does maintenance work later on, they will know what you've done, and when.

You close the lid and move on to the next box. You go through the same process with the system within that box. One by one you move through all the boxes, making each of the unique systems within them perfect, closing the lids afterward.

It indeed takes the entire day to complete your work. Once you've finished, you take a last look around the room. The boxes are in neat rows, their lids closed, and you are confident the systems within each box are working perfectly. You know the department's output will now be very, very good because each of its systems is working flawlessly. How could it be otherwise? You also know the new department manager will be system-improvement oriented, watching over things, not allowing the systems to fall back into disarray. There will be routine maintenance. As you walk away, you feel intensely satisfied with your work and with yourself.

There it is—the *Work the System* process of seeing the world as a collection of systems that are, one by one, isolated and made perfect, and once perfected, routinely managed for maintenance and upgrading.

Here's the no-brainer that eludes most people: In the course of a day and in the course of a life, each movement we make is a single step in a linear sequence of steps intended to accomplish something. *Each thing we do is a component of a system.*

We are not balls in a pinball machine randomly bouncing around at the mercy of our surroundings.

My intention in part one has been to present illustrations and evidence from a variety of angles so you will see the systems of your own life on a visceral level. I'm being repetitive, hammering things home. Are you "there" yet? If not, be patient as I belabor the elements of the new perspective while slowly introducing the how-tos.

If you don't experience the aha! moment soon, it's okay. The fake-it-'til-you-make-it routine can get you there.

THE FIRST STEP: MAKE YOUR SYSTEMS VISIBLE

You know this by now. First, make the various systems consciously visible. Second, one at a time, bring them to the foreground for examination. Third, adjust them. Fourth, document them. Fifth, maintain them.

By plucking individual systems out of the amorphous mass of your real-time existence—that intense, swirling fracas of sights, sounds, and events that is your life—you can examine and then precisely manipulate the workings of those systems. But first you must see them.

Reaching the point where you *see* the systems around you is the first and most significant step. It's a mini-enlightenment. When the epiphany occurs, you will have internalized the premise that *systems make up your life*, and you will know that asserting control of them is management at the most fundamental level. You will view the world with new clarity, as a logical collection of individual processes. Details will be sharper and more vivid, the colors more vibrant.

Moment by moment, in real time, you will proceed through your day seeing everything around you as part of a system. No more will you perceive your world as a random conglomeration of people, objects, and situations. You'll see life as a logical collection of individual processes.

What seemed complex will suddenly appear elementary.

With confidence in your new vision, you will change your strategy from fire-killing to system improvement because it is obvious this is the most sensible thing to do.

YOU MUST STAND OUTSIDE OF IT

If you want to see where you fit in the machine that is your life, you must observe it from an external vantage point. *You must stand outside of it if you are to see how you are a part of it.*

There is nothing shadowy in this. This is simply about seeing things in a different way. Remember, however, that this mind-set is different from the mental posture most people pack around. Instead of seeing yourself as an internal component of circumstances, you are an observer from above as you watch yourself down there in the middle of it all. You see things clearly and reach down to control your every movement, almost as if you were a child playing with a tiny action figure.

You are the child and the toy is your life.

There is no need for me to list a one-through-ten-step process for making the *Work the System* method produce results in your life: You must simply "get" the new perspective of seeing the systems in your life with the same clarity with which you see the rest of the physical world around you. Once that happens, the rest will be fill-in-the-blanks sensibility.

Again, here's how you will see your world: The day's happenings are visible as individual elements, arranged in logical sequences. It's borderline metaphysical as you hover above your world. You are the "watcher," the observer of your life.

Your day is spent working on your systems. These are "one-time" tasks as you make each system perfect, one by one. Over time, self-confidence replaces confusion. Your systems—business, personal, mechanical—hum along. You gaze down at your handiwork and feel an intense self-respect. You are proud of what you have accomplished.

Considering your new mind-set, you think, "Why couldn't I see this before?" You look back on your previous life and observe that embroiled in minutiae as you were, you were blind to the systems that lay beneath your comings and goings. You remember the day when the shroud lifted, when sequential life systems became visible and your perception of the world's workings shifted. You also remember the first inklings of the potency of systems methodology and how soon it proved itself in action: Tangible rewards came quickly. You remember that removing the shroud didn't take a whole lot of faith or hard work, just some quiet observation.

Acquiring the *Work the System* posture is a transformation. You can look forward with anticipation because the moment of shift is an intuitive leap. It will be the consummate insight, the singular event that changes everything. The day you "get it" is a day you will remember. My prediction is that this will happen soon, possibly before you finish this book. Maybe it grips you now.

IT'S WHAT YOU DO

Now you know, and thus you will act. Consider the following points:

First, *it's what one DOES that counts.* Good intentions and a positive attitude are not enough. What matters is the action one takes, right here in the tangible world.

Second, *getting things right most of the time is good enough.* The part that doesn't come out well is just part of the overhead: the cost of doing business, of taking risks, of external confusion, of coping with a changing world that is sometimes one step ahead of your best efforts, of being alive. As by-products of your advancement forward, accept that less-than-perfect events are going to happen. Three steps forward, one step back, is the way it goes.

Third, remember that *most people don't fail by making overt mistakes.* They fail because they don't take action. If you fall into this category, prepare to change your ways.

YOUR DAY WILL NEVER BE THE SAME

It is incredibly satisfying to have control, to have things make sense, and to determine your own destiny. And you'll become tenacious about this new direction because the improvements come fast and strong.

I belabor this point because it is key: *Once the Work the System methodology is internalized and applied, you will be a different person.* No more feeling anxious in the morning, your head filling with encroaching worries even before you get out of bed. During the day, no more long hours spent killing fires. No more evenings spent buried in paperwork or sitting exhausted, zombie-like in front of the TV, with no hope of relief tomorrow.

Instead, at the end of the day you look back and see that you spent your time immersed in one-time creative projects and productive conversations with staff, customers, friends, and family. You feel gratification that the past day's efforts were further incremental steps toward even more freedom and prosperity. You don't pine for the "big break" because it's clear the big break is already occurring piece by piece, step by step. In control from dawn to dusk, you know you are building your destiny in a solid and honorable way.

You not only made incremental progress toward your most important goals, you also spent time with the people who matter most to you and you did the things that gave you pleasure. There's plenty enough money now, and your circle of influence is growing.

You are happy with yourself. You know why your life has improved, why you feel in control. It's because of you: *You did that to you!*

The *Work the System* process is not magical. It's logical. You can see the cause-and-effect of your own actions. The *Work the System* mind-set will keep you ever alert to small system improvements that can easily be implemented. If you can see the systems, you can make them better.

 ### Violating a Social System

In Italy, Linda and I stayed in a small guesthouse in the tiny coastal town of Monterosso. One morning, I sat alone at a breakfast table in the corner of the dining room. Other tourists surrounded me, quietly enjoying their cappuccinos and pastries. I worked on my laptop, putting the final touches on this book, my breakfast dishes pushed aside.

The manager of the guesthouse approached me, and in halting English she asked, "Are you finished with your breakfast?"

I answered, "Si."

Then she said, "Please. To work, take your computer to the lobby downstairs. This is a place of breakfast."

That odd phrasing—*"This is a place of breakfast"*—was perfect. In her wonderfully nuanced English, my host got directly to the point and I instantly understood. There was no quibbling with the logic. I was working in "a place of breakfast," and working there was wrong. Italians consider eating a semisacred process that should not be sullied with work. My incursion was callous; I was not respecting a system that had been operating for scores of generations.

I moved downstairs to the lobby, a place where many things—including a too-busy American with his laptop—were allowed.

I understand how Europeans sometimes consider Americans crass and overbearing. It was a humbling, outside-and-slightly-elevated reminder that I must respect the systems of others.

Are there social situations where it seems things don't "click"? For instance, have you inadvertently disrupted a conversation, which in itself was a kind of a virtual system between two other people? How does it feel to be interrupted when you are deeply involved in a phone conversation, book, or some complex detail of your work?

PART TWO

CRITICAL DOCUMENTATION

CHAPTER 8

Swallowing the Horse Pill

Why aren't you going to step up to do something about it?
Don't you feel there are enough live people passing off
as dead people already?

—Anonymous

Note that having your protocols written down is at least as important as what you say. This section describes the fundamentals of *Work the System* documentation. They are presented here as we use them at Centratel but readers are welcome to copy and customize them. To create your version of these documents, use our *Work the System Easy Template*™ software package. Go to workthesystem.com/easy for details.

Linda came up with the following analogy for the three *Work the System* documents. The Strategic Objective is your Declaration of Independence, your mandate for a better future. The General Operating Principles document is your Constitution, a set of guidelines for future decision making. The Working Procedures are your laws, the rules of your game. Can you imagine our government not having its foundation recorded in written form? Why would it be any different for your business or your job—or your life?

First you will create the Strategic Objective, then the Operating Principles. These documents establish your bearing; they will keep you sailing straight. Producing them won't take long.

Then you will begin your Working Procedures, and it is here that you will spend most of your time. Again, the improvement of a system is a system improvement, and the documentation of that system improvement is called a Working Procedure.

TIME AND EFFORT

One day not long after the systems-perspective lightbulb switched on in my head, I had another insight. It dawned on me that creating the necessary documentation would not be flashy. The process would sometimes be tedious, and it was clear that documenting all of our systems would take time. The Working Procedures would not fall into place as easily as the first two controlling documents, the Strategic Objective and the General Operating Principles. Nevertheless, it would be a mandatory undertaking.

Firsthand I saw that within my own TAS industry, few owners/managers perceive their businesses from an outside-and-slightly-elevated perspective. Instead, they thrash within the inner workings, smacking those moles on the head. I realized immediately that my industry was not unique: Few small businesses document their direction, and still fewer document their processes.

Why is that? I thought. If this systems methodology is so simple and so potent, why aren't more small-business owners doing it? Could it be because the system-improvement work is too much of a challenge? Too hard, too labor intensive? It's all of those things! And the sheer unassuming nature of what must be done, combined with the fact that other small-business owners don't do it, is smoking-gun evidence of its viability! In itself, this revelation gave me a surge of excitement about the documentation chores that lay ahead.

In any case, if I was to establish solid direction, hone processes to near perfection, and then expect those processes to continue to be near perfect in the future, it was logical the direction and processes would have to be written down. And then—there was no getting away from it—the next prosaic task would be to ensure that my staff precisely followed the documentation.

My next moves were obvious, but creating the documentation would take time away from the ongoing efforts of keeping the business afloat from day to day. Business demands would not step aside while we improved systems and wrote up the attending documentation, and I wondered if we could find the time to write everything down. But then I realized this was a moot question. Accomplishing the work was mandatory because if we didn't do it the company would fail—and my guess was that if we *did* do it, the company would flourish. So I swallowed the gigantic horse pill that there was some serious work to do—unexciting documentation work— and plunged ahead full steam.

Motivating Yourself

To get off the mark, remember there will never be an "easy button" you can push to make everything instantly better. Documenting systems takes time and focus. But you are already working hard and long, so what's the big deal? Tell yourself simply that you must continue to work hard for just a bit longer.

PREPARATION LEADS TO BETTER CONTROL

Yes, the system-improvement documentation, the one-time heavy lifting, will be intensive at first, but once it's in place, the ongoing work will dramatically decrease. (In my case, I transformed hundred-hour workweeks into two-hour workweeks.)

A primary thrust of the *Work the System* method is to generate extra time so you can better prepare. Proper preparation leads to better control of future events, which leads to higher efficiency. Higher efficiency produces more available time—and some of that available time is reinvested in additional preparation.

This is the opposite of a cycle of diminishing returns. Again, it's the cycle of *increasing* returns, a circular system that builds upon itself to ever-higher positive results.

The largest obstacle to better preparation is the reluctance to invest the necessary time to be better prepared! At the beginning, even if you have experienced the insight that systems make up everything in your life, you must be patient and self-disciplined. You must keep your head down and grind out those Working Procedures until prosperity and free time begin to arrive, thus confirming deep down in your belly that *Work the System* preparation is a smart thing to do. When the results begin to materialize—and it won't take long—you will become a fanatic for documentation.

Note that some documentation will be useful in your personal life, but it will be informal and less intensive.

Here is a summary of the *Work the System* documentation you will put together.

1. **Strategic Objective.** The one-page Strategic Objective document will provide overall direction for your business and your personal life. You will create this document yourself. It won't take more than six to eight hours to complete. (Caution: This is not a job for a committee. It's a job for you, the leader.) Once it's completed, you will get feedback from your superiors, your peers, and your staff. Over time, you will tweak it as necessary. As the years pass, it won't change much. (In appendix B you will find Centratel's Strategic Objective.) Create a separate one for your personal life.

2. **General Operating Principles.** Upon completion of the Strategic Objective, you will begin to put together a collection of written General Operating Principles. Just two or three pages long, this condensed "guidelines for decision making" document requires ten to twenty hours to complete, but these hours will be spread over a period of a month or two. (Yes, the composition of this document is also a job for *you*, although you will want to get input from others.) You will extract these principles from your everyday experience while formulating them from the perspective of your new systems mind-set. These principles are what you believe, and new ones will surface unannounced. Avoid rushing the list. Be thoughtful and patient with yourself; put them together carefully and your written principles will change little over the years. Write a thorough document for your business; it can be more informal for your personal life. (Centratel's documented 30 Principles are in appendix C.)

3. **Working Procedures.** Instead of killing fires, you will spend time creating a fireproof environment. Your Working Procedures will be the nitty-gritty, blue-collar fundamentals of your work. This documentation is your specific collection of protocols that outline exactly how the systems of your business or your job will operate. (Working Procedures are not necessary for your personal life although the concept should travel with you everywhere.) Brief, concise, and authored by you and other key people (your staff, peers, supervisors), 95 percent of your procedures will follow the same 1-2-3-step format. The other 5 percent will follow an open, "narrative" format.

Every system improvement you make will have its own written Working Procedure. As you did with the General Operating Principles, you will begin creating your procedures just after you complete your Strategic Objective. You will start with the most troublesome critical systems and then work down through dozens if not hundreds of additional systems, depending on the complexity of your business, job, or profession. But, over this period, it won't be a full-time job. If you have staff, use your best people to do the majority of this legwork. Foundational to your everyday business experience and adjusted with evolving circumstances, Working Procedures are the fluid part of the *Work the System* method. (Centratel's "Procedure for Procedures" is noted in appendix D.)

Lifestyle Requirements

If we choose to live a certain lifestyle, that lifestyle has certain requirements. There are tasks that *must* be accomplished. These are task *requirements*, not "when-I-get-around-to-it tasks" or "if-I-feel-like-it tasks." To achieve your desired lifestyle, you must accomplish these tasks no matter your disposition at the moment. The ability to get the job done—no matter the current frame of mind—is necessary for success. No matter how onerous the job, or how little you want to do what is required, the payoff will arrive as long as you take the steps! You do not have to like the steps you must take. You just have to take them. Nine out of ten people don't understand this. They think, rather, "If I don't enjoy what I am doing, then what I am doing is incorrect." Bad presumption.

The documents you will create are mechanical aids. However, something else is important about them. They are tangible. It makes what you are doing and where you are going real. With written documentation, you can put your hands on your work and your future. Every day you will see your methodology and goals, and this will be a reminder to stay on the path. Always remember that surging thoughts, desires, and hopes are intangibles and they can divert you. Documentation, however, is real, and it will keep you straight. Once you begin to get things down on paper, this will become obvious.

Your controlling documents do not have to be perfect in the first drafts. They can be grammatically incorrect, the sentence structure can be less than perfect, and they can be brief. What is important is that you begin to create and use your documentation. Just begin! You can clean it up later. It is critically important to be self-disciplined from the beginning—and this self-discipline will be evident in just getting started.

THE DOWN TIMES: GET OUTSIDE YOURSELF

The Strategic Objective, General Operating Principles, and Working Procedures are your self-created guiding lights. In the tough times, they remind you that you are a system-of-systems and that tweaking certain external and internal subsystems is what you must do. When you are not feeling strong and your emotions are negative, your guidelines are right there, ready to get you back on track, or at least keep you from straying too far. As Mick Jagger said, "It's all right letting yourself go as long as you can get yourself back."

Create your controlling documents in moments of lucidity when your thinking is clear and you have a firm grip on the unadulterated truths of your life. The self-discipline of today will pay off later when you are not so strong. For example, when you realize you are watching your temporary depression from the outside, you will know you have reached a higher level of control. This is cognitive self-management, the ability to examine and adjust your thoughts from an external vantage point. You see your thoughts as independent of you, systems unto themselves: singular, tangible entities, just like any of the other systems under your control.

Your systems perspective will remind you that the reasons for the down times are often simple things: too little sleep, low blood sugar, excessive work or TV, negative people, a gloomy environment, the payback for ingesting a mood-altering substance, and so on. Get outside these influences and see them for what they are. Minimize them and they will no longer eat away at self-control and progress. They will no longer drain your energy or create depression.

In my own life, being tired drives me downhill faster than anything else. Like clockwork, every day between 1:00 p.m. and 2:00 p.m. I go into a physical and mental downturn, and I either nap it off or I crawl through the afternoon, understanding that my physical body—and my thinking process—is at low ebb. By 4:00 p.m. I am fine again. Discover your own cycles and work with them.

STORMS OF THE CRIMINAL MIND

The criminal mind has a certain grasp of the mechanics of the world, sometimes more so than the average law-abiding citizen. In the classic, colloquial sense, the criminal "works the system," as he or she strips away the niceties, examines the raw mechanisms of the world's workings, and without concern for others, manipulates those mechanisms to selfish benefit. Yes, the criminal approaches things with a malefic bent, but one can't deny that the viewpoint is outside and slightly elevated.

Nevertheless, criminality is a losing game because it violates overarching societal systems. If we consider society as a primary system, criminality is nothing less than a flaw, and the primary system works hard to eliminate that flaw one way or the other. If you are a criminal, the force is *not* with you.

Consider the plight of the chronic lawbreaker who gyrates outside of things, bucking accepted notions of how one should act. For selfish reasons, the criminal directs energy toward personal gain without regard for the accepted rules of the primary system—society—taking shortcuts, exploiting system elements, and making small-time gains. As the system is bucked and manipulated without regard for fairness and compassion— the bulwarks of a just society—personal pain arrives in an overt way: jail time, for instance, or in a more covert lack of personal peace. The criminal is afloat in a stormy sea. The TV series *The Sopranos* perfectly illustrated the paranoia of "fighting the system." The characters were diabolical and tormented, and ultimately doomed.

If one is working "outside the system," what is the solution? It is to make the decision to accept the general human process as it is; to play the game as it's laid out—to follow the rules. Things are just smoother that way. In the free world there is a lot of latitude to fit into things and to get ahead in business, social networks, and personal relationships. One has unlimited options to succeed without breaking the rules. The universe welcomes manipulation if it results in a better, more-efficient system, but it will fight manipulation that is disruptive.

HOW IT WORKS

Look forward to this: In the midst of a less-than-perfect day, you will watch yourself drag your emotions out of a black hole rather than allowing them to swallow you up. You will see yourself do this from your outside-and-slightly-elevated vantage point. Later, you will see it happen again, and then later, again. These self-rescues incrementally strengthen control, and after a while you will expect this even-keeled response. Soon you will find you won't be so inclined to resort to the old antidote of avoidance; no longer will you bludgeon your way through the downtimes with over-work, alcohol, coffee, sugar, or drugs, the things that rescue your mood in the moment but guarantee more intense downtimes in the future.

The learning cycle will continue upward until you have a solid grip on your world and you realize your Strategic Objective, General Operating Principles, and Working Procedures have pushed you to become one of those rare individuals whose backbone is made of steel. It seems odd that dispassionate documentation could have this kind of effect, but as you can see, there is much more to this than the written word.

EMOTIONAL FLUCTUATIONS

Like bedrock, your three controlling documents will stand against the storms that blow across your world. And what storms create the most havoc, slowing, halting, or reversing forward progress? Your own emotions.

Documentation lays out everything that is important for getting you to a place of control in your life: your goals and how you will achieve them; your beliefs about how things work; what is most important to you; and how you will operate. Because of it, your forward progress will ebb only slightly as you encounter the unpredictable and inevitable emotional surges that are part of the human condition. With the *Work the System* methodology in place, you will minimize the impact of your negative emotional fluctuations. It may be slower progress in those times, but it will be progress.

No matter what, there will be times when you think you are sinking. Nonetheless, when those times happen, your documentation will reach down and yank you to the surface before you drown.

OUTSIDE AND SLIGHTLY ELEVATED

At Centratel, when we took action from our new external stance, turmoil evaporated, to be replaced by order. Once we began the new methodology, it was easy to continue because positive results accumulated quickly. The more we invested in system improvement and attending documentation— working the system—the more positive the results we experienced.

Centratel is highly profitable now, and I spend little time managing it because the business is self-propelling. As project engineer, I watch over things from a distance, nudging here and there to keep the business traveling in a straight line and at full speed. Centratel is not under control because of my presence as a detail chaser. It's under control because of my insistence on perfecting the systems that compose it. Of course, another critical element of our success is my staff's enthusiasm for the method they helped put into place. They are project engineers, too.

First you work your systems.
Then your systems do the work.

Centratel is a pleasant place to work. Calm efficiency pervades every aspect of the company. Concurrent with the enormous improvements at my business, the systems perspective flows through my personal life, and I have the same levels of control and freedom there, too. I regained my health years ago and today consider myself more than robust. One might think my adoption of the new systems perspective came about because I was courageous. But that wasn't the case. It was fear and exhaustion. It took impending doom to see life was not going to conform to my wishes just because I thought it should.

Why weren't the answers obvious to me *before* there was a gun to my head? Part of the reason was that although the year-to-year struggle was killing me, it was more comfortable—more convenient—to acquiesce to predictable day-to-day pain than to question my overall vision and methodology.

There was also arrogance: It was easier to posture myself as a hero, facing and then overcoming incredible external odds, doggedly marching on, rather than to question my presumption that the world would someday get a clue and adjust to my personal requirements. But when catastrophe was finally upon me, everything distilled down to the raw indisputable fact that I was not managing the systems of my life.

Am I happy the insight came as the end result of trauma? If that was what was required, yes. Do you have to have a gun-to-the-head experience to get to the same place? No!

Late that night, nine years ago when the lightbulb in my head finally flicked on, it struck me that although there was some work to do, it would be maddeningly simple to repair my business and my life: All I had to do was identify systems, isolate them, and then fix them one at a time! Does this make sense now? Do you see there is no need to undergo a cataclysm in order to change your perspective and then fix things?

In retrospect, the almost humorous aspect of my outside-and-slightly-elevated enlightenment was the realization this was not some kind of divine blessing bestowed upon me alone. The systems perspective is already permanently etched into the minds of those who manage large, successful organizations everywhere. Yet many of the people who innately embrace the systems perspective, as simple a concept as it is, can't describe it much less identify it as the critical factor of their success.

System Questions

By dispassionately dealing with stone-cold reality, the odds of getting what you want are infinitely higher than waiting for a ghost to communicate good tidings, a horoscope or tarot cards to predict a prosperous future, or the multimillion-dollar lottery landing in your lap. Be mechanical. Can you imagine how you will feel as you watch yourself get a grip on life and create what you want due to your own actions, not because of improbable fate, magic, dumb luck, or someone else's benevolence?

There are system questions—system filters—you can pose to enable you to really see the hard and cold reality of any given situation. Ask, "Without regard for my personal preference, what exactly is going on here?" Carry that question around with you everywhere, and when the necessary action is obvious, but you are still hesitant, ask, "Is not wanting to take action in this moment enough of a reason to NOT take action?"

FLOW

You will watch in fascination as the world's endless systems ripple on. It is nothing less than flow, and you'll like seeing it, being part of it. You will view your personal existence from this nearly metaphysical systems perspective that is a step away and a little bit above events. In your work and your personal life, your job will be to tweak your systems, gently goading each to more and more efficiency. (Regarding systems that are outside of your control, you will make no attempts at adjustment because it is a waste of time and energy.)

This world operates at 99.9 percent efficiency because there are unalterable physical laws that are powered by an unfathomable strength—a strength that hungers for order and efficiency. In the systems that make up our lives, results occur in a cold-blooded way; outcomes don't mysteriously conform to our personal desires just because we want them to. But this is a good thing because this mechanical reality is predictable; it is something we can depend upon and therefore confidently use to our own benefit. Think about that shovel in the garage. Do you ever question it won't dig a hole? And that rope? There is no question it will secure something, if that is your need. Conversely, will you ever attempt to dig a hole with the rope? The certainty you feel in answering these questions is the same certainty you will feel for the larger mechanics of the world, of the machinations that you will see are predictable and reliable once you "get" the systems mind-set.

When you understand the relentless dependability of reality's mechanics, and then carefully "work" those mechanics, you will get what you want.

THREE LARGE STEPS AHEAD

In the middle of my business and health rejuvenation, I was pounded hard by two unexpected, earthshaking blows. One was the nasty legal battle mentioned earlier. The other was a bone-crushing personal family loss. Those two nightmares arrived at the same time. The first lasted two years; the second continued until recently. It was painful during those dark times, but I was able to roll through the days with sanity and effectiveness, watching the goings-on from my outside-and-slightly-elevated vantage point.

In chapter one I asserted several points I want to repeat here. The *Work the System* mind-set is different from the mental posture most people pack around from day to day. Instead of seeing yourself as an internal component of circumstances, enmeshed within the day's swirling events, your *Work the System* vantage point is "outside and slightly elevated" from those events. The day's happenings are visible as separate and individual elements, arranged in logical sequences. You are an observer looking down on things, examining the comings and goings of the day as if they are tangible, physical objects. Things are simple and understandable. Wherever you look, the machinations of the world make sense: Step-by-step, one thing leads to another as the systems around you continuously execute. You constantly work on those systems. You make them better, one by one. Over time, complexity and confusion decrease to be replaced by order, calm, and rock-solid self-confidence. There is little fire-killing and little confusion, and as you continue to peer down at your handiwork, you feel an intense self-respect and you are proud of what you've accomplished.

Does this make more sense now?

Once you "get it," the *Work the System* mind-set is natural and unforced. Here is how it will be: You wake up in the morning with an immediate focus on what is most important for the day ahead. The tasks you will accomplish will be one-time, creative efforts, each aimed at carrying you closer to the objectives outlined in your two Strategic Objective documents—one for your business, one for your personal life. Although you will minimize stepping backward, there is no avoiding it because that is what getting through the day includes. You accept those imperfect movements as part of the overhead that comes with the much more significant forward movement— three large steps ahead for every one small step back. And the inevitable earthquakes? You'll be ready.

And at the end of the day, you feel satisfied because there has been tangible advancement toward your prime personal objectives. Working or relaxing, you don't float or obsess anymore. You direct, build, watch, and enjoy. It flows.

The Giant Machine

Deep in the hills of northern Italy, the world's largest manufacturer of computer printers keeps a factory running 24/7/365. The mechanical and electronic workers don't take breaks, and they work their entire lives in this fixed location. A daily line of transport trucks delivers raw materials and picks up fully packaged products. A few cars in the tiny parking lot indicate there is merely a small contingent of human workers present.

Given the proper security clearances, issued from the lone security guard minding the gate, a brave person can walk through the center of this giant machine. Doing so, one quickly learns that even human visitors are under the system's control. Standing at one end of this "system of systems," one can barely make out the other end. It's a huge *machine*, as wide as it is long. Approaching a well-defined walkway, the human intruder is warned by red flashing lights to stop while a part of the mechanical line physically retracts in order to allow passage. Once the visitor passes, the track closes and the machine continues at a somewhat accelerated pace to make up for the time lost by the intrusion.

This is not the place for the faint of heart or the claustrophobic, as there are no escape routes. Should the machine fail to detect your presence, there are no humans readily available to intervene on your behalf. Yes, you are free to leave but only at the mercy of the system and only at a pace that doesn't interfere with system requirements.

The giant machine is made up of subassemblies, and those subassemblies cooperate with each other until complete products are rolling off the end of the line. The fully tested printers are packaged and shipped to a local store near you, and in all likelihood the first human hands to touch the printers are those of retail purchasers.

This is a system of systems with a clear goal—the production of things of value. And where are the human masters? Outside and slightly elevated, of course, monitoring, adjusting, and maintaining.

Think about the "giant machines" of your life—for instance, a car or a house—each standing alone and pretty much taking care of itself. Can you think of others that make life easier, especially in the workplace?

CHAPTER 9

We Are Project Engineers

Management works in the system;
leadership works on the system.

—STEPHEN COVEY

AS AN AD-HOC SYNOPSIS—by now you know how much I like to review things, to drill them home—the essence of the *Work the System* method is to

1. Internalize the fundamental, outside-and-slightly-elevated system -improvement perspective.

2. Pinpoint and describe goals for your business, job, and life. Briefly define the general methods you will use to achieve those goals. This is your Strategic Objective.

3. Create your personal collection of General Operating Principles. Use them to control decision making.

4. Define specific systems for improvement, including the ones that exist and the ones you must create. Be ready to discard others.

5. Dissect each system into its most fundamental components. For your business or your job, describe each system on paper in a 1-2-3-step format.

6. Improve the efficiency of the component steps, one system at a time and leaning hard toward stark simplicity. Change sequences

and add or delete steps as necessary. Make each of your systems perfect.

7. Document each system into a Working Procedure in order to ensure the continuity of your systems for your business or your job. (Working Procedures are not necessary for your nonwork life.)

8. Put the new Working Procedures into play and tend to them on a regular basis, inspecting and tweaking as necessary.

YOUR PERSONAL ANALOGY

In step one, internalizing the system-improvement perspective is mandatory. Without this visceral grasp, subsequent steps two through eight just won't happen in your real, mechanical world. The strength to take a new direction comes more from a belief lodged in the belly rather than from something new learned in the head.

To really grasp the system-improvement perspective, it is useful to create a personal system analogy, a "systems template," that you find personally meaningful. Your analogy will illustrate systems methodology to *you*. In your day-to-day existence, you will keep this analogy in mind in order to keep your systems perspective front and center and to remind you of the characteristics that all systems share. A vivid personal system analogy is the antidote to a too-busy day: that is, a day that ruthlessly attempts to divert your attention from the system-improvement process to the wasteful act of fire-killing. The analogy will keep you on target.

You want your analogy to be personally believable. Its mechanical basis must be something you don't question. Also, it is essential to find one that is easy to visualize as separate from its surroundings, one that can stand on its own.

If you are in medicine, bodily systems offer myriad possibilities. You can draw examples from organ function, skeletal structure, or recovery from injury.

If you sell cars, consider the conveyor belt of an auto plant, or a car itself with all of its subsystems and how they must be monitored and tweaked to stay at peak efficiency.

As a firefighter, think about the equipment and procedures that must function efficiently no matter what.

A pilot has the preflight checklist, which is a terrific example of examining an existing system for flaws while ensuring that all subsystems are at peak efficiency. The airplane itself, or even a single flight, is a great system analogy as the aircraft automatically conducts directional micro-adjustments, confirms subsystems are functional, and warns of system dysfunction.

Your analogy will keep your energies channeled toward system management as it reminds you that a jumble of fire-killing will drag you down. Your analogy will be a steady reminder that you are a project engineer who creates and maintains efficient systems, not a fire-killer who responds to crisis after crisis.

The analogy will help you enormously at the beginning. Later, it will be an occasional pleasant reflection of who you are, where you stand, and how you get through the day.

As an illustration, the following is the analogy I use. As you read, start to think of one that fits your own world. No, you don't have to put it down on paper.

THE NEW-SERVICE FACILITATOR

My personal analogy is about electricity: how it reaches people in their homes and businesses, and my past role as an electric utility project engineer.

Power line circuits perfectly illustrate the mechanics of the *Work the System* methodology to *me*, so this is my analogy of a closed system. It is easy for me to visualize an electricity distribution system as a separate, unique entity and not one in which surrounding complexities of the world infringe. It's my personal, perfect illustration of the mechanics of linear systems everywhere.

When I was twenty-eight, I took a job in the engineering department of a rural electric utility near my home in Central Oregon. The utility is one of the largest Rural Electrification Administration (REA) co-ops in the United States, with thousands of miles of power lines branching throughout the Central Oregon region and serving tens of thousands of residential, commercial, and agricultural customers.

Of all co-ops in the United States, my REA co-op's operations and engineering personnel experience the most extreme environmental, meteorological, and socioeconomic challenges. On the same day, linemen can face both mountain snowstorms and desert heat; vertical mountain pitches and long river crossings; high-density city construction and remote rural troubleshooting.

For the first half of my seven-year stint with the co-op, my job title was "new-service facilitator."

As one of the co-op's four new-service facilitators, I met with contractors and landowners who were about to build homes. My task was to arrange for our construction crews to "tap" into the nearest existing power line in order to extend new electric service to the customer's construction site. Usually, the distance from the power line to the site was fewer than a hundred yards.

I examined the new home site, found the closest power pole, and wrote up instructions and a list of materials for the construction crews so they could get the electricity delivered to the customer via low-voltage overhead and underground cable.

My job had little to do with the primary electrical system. My area of responsibility was outside the massive power-generating dams that created the electricity far to the north on the Columbia River, and outside the thousands of miles of high-voltage power lines and associated complex equipment that distributes electricity in bulk throughout the region. My task was to establish small power line extensions to individual new customers by designing small subsystems. These subsystems were simple additions to my utility's massive "electricity distribution network," the primary system.

I filled this position as new-service facilitator for three years. Then I got a promotion. The promotion moved me from the periphery of the system to the heart of it, where I would have a much greater impact on the primary system itself, and on the many customers it served.

My new job title was "project engineer," a perfect description of my new role (and in your new role, it will be your title too, so pay attention here). I would be responsible for designing and supervising the construction of large, high-voltage "distribution feeders" into whole subdivisions, as well as working on complex "system-improvement" projects that

affected thousands of customers at a time. It was also my job to keep an eye on large segments of the primary electrical system in order to spot problems and to recommend improvements. There was the necessary overall maintenance, too. System components aged and the environment changed, and it was my job to monitor these variables and recommend repairs and upgrades.

In short, my job was to analyze portions of the main electrical distribution system, design improvements, and then pass those designs on to the construction crews.

I put my designs down on paper using a precise format. The goal was to be thorough yet concise; to give the construction crews the information they needed—no more and no less—so they could proceed quickly through the construction work.

Note how the analogy describes my transition from handling small and isolated add-on tasks to large internal system-improvement projects. Also note there were strict design and documentation protocols.

FLIRTING WITH THE NEW PERSPECTIVE

My previous position and my new position had an important commonality. In each case, when I went to work, from the beginning of the day to the end of the day, I was focused on the co-op's electrical system. While I was on the job, the system stood separate from the rest of the world. Sure I took breaks, had lunch, and made a personal phone call now and then, but all-in-all, the electricity distribution system—the network of poles and wire—was paramount in my consciousness, standing out in my mind as its own entity, separate and distinct from my children, my finances, my politics. When I was on the job, the electricity distribution system had my focused attention as if nothing else existed. And it was not just separate in my mind, it was that way in reality, a primary system inserted into the world as an independent entity, spreading its tentacles as it fulfilled its singular purpose of delivering electricity to lots of people.

At the end of the day, as I returned home to pay attention to the other systems of my life, I changed my perspective as if I had flipped a switch. I didn't consciously notice this daily transition (and little did I know that I was toying with the outside-and-slightly-elevated perspective that would form the basis of this book.

If you are like most people, you are in that same place, with an unconscious tendency to dissect complexities so the exposed elements can be dealt with one at a time. The *Work the System* method will turn that soft, ephemeral tendency into an assertive, structured quest—an everyday pilgrimage to "work" the systems that compose your world.

SYSTEM MANAGEMENT

With the promotion at the co-op, my role morphed from designing small subsystems for individual customers to making system improvements in the primary electrical system that served thousands of customers. Instead of adding to the primary electrical system in bits and pieces, I was managing large segments to ensure that it continued to provide an uninterrupted supply of electricity to large numbers of customers. I tweaked and coddled the primary system to keep it strong and efficient.

Notice I was not climbing the poles or stringing wire. My job was to devise system improvements that would make the primary electrical system more robust, and then to oversee the implementation of those system improvements by other people. This is a crucial point of the analogy.

All of this was "system management." I was unconsciously "working the system," and this management process would later insert itself into all parts of my life as I came to understand the logic of it. Today, my former role serves me well as an analogy—a template—for how I want to visualize all aspects of my life. Like my position as project engineer with the electric utility years ago, today I examine, tweak, maintain, and upgrade all the systems of my existence, while I avoid getting caught up in minor add-ons.

I no longer "major in minors." Your own analogy will remind you to avoid that, too.

MAINTENANCE AND 99.9 PERCENT RELIABILITY

In any part of life, in order to avoid system failures and to ensure top efficiency, the performance of regular system maintenance is mandatory. Now that you understand that systems are everywhere, it will make sense to you that maintenance of all human systems is necessary: changing the car's oil, conducting staff meetings, watering the houseplants, dinner out with a spouse, ball games with the kids, bonuses for the best employees, routine visits with customers, record keeping, physical fitness, etc. However, for many people in the midst of chaos control, skipping these important "wheel greasing" chores is the first casualty. In so many life situations that include careers, marriages, friendships, mechanical devices, play, homes, personal health—all of it—the necessary routine maintenance is skipped because of fire-killing, simple laziness, and, especially, ignorance of the way linear systems proceed in the real, mechanical world.

Electricity originates from a generating facility and then power lines carry it to the end user. For the electricity, it's a long, hazard-wrought trip through multiple electrical subsystems and tough terrain. Weather extremes, vandalism, and the incessant ravages of time imperil the electricity's delivery. Yet, interestingly, in checking official statistics at the utility where I used to work, I found that over the last seven years, the average customer's power failed an average of just 73 minutes per year. Wow! Think about that. There are 525,600 minutes in a year, which means the average electric utility customer had steady electric power more than 99.9 percent of the time. Does that percentage sound familiar?

In considering a power line's path through hundreds of miles of hostile environment, combined with the volatile high-voltage electricity itself, which is so anxious to escape its confining wires and transformers, how do the management and staff of an electric utility accomplish this astonishing degree of reliability? They do it by viewing their electrical network as a system that must be assertively and relentlessly maintained, not just a conglomeration of poles, wire, and equipment that receives attention only when things go wrong. The people employed by the electric company start by designing and installing a robust electrical system, and then they coddle it.

THE HEART OF THE ANALOGY

In summary, my role as project engineer on a large electrical system was to isolate the electrical system and then look down on it from an outside-and-slightly-elevated vantage point in order to:

1. Design system improvements;

2. Create new subsystems from scratch while eliminating ones that are obsolete; and

3. Monitor existing systems to make sure they function reliably in a changing, demanding environment.

What's your analogy? A car, a human body, an airplane, a ship? Use it to remind yourself to view your world with the system perspective. See the perfection of your encapsulated system analogy and apply it to whatever situation you find yourself in. You can do this because, for practical purposes, all the systems of the world operate in exactly the same way. This is not theory and there is no mystery. This is mechanical reality.

WATCH THINGS FROM A DISTANCE

As I visualize an electrical power system as a metaphor for my life, it is a reminder to avoid being a worker and to be, rather, a project engineer. As you apply your own analogy to your business or supervisory job, you will find yourself deflecting hands-on work to others. Instead, you will be creating new systems, designing improvements on existing systems, and supervising the people who do the actual work. Of course, if you are an artist or other creator, or you work for someone else, this will not be entirely true. However, whatever your life's role, there is room for movement in the *Work the System* direction—a direction that can only improve your situation, whatever it is. (More on the job and work aspect in chapter 19.)

In considering your new analogy, and from your new posture as a project engineer, you will begin to watch things from a distance, from that place that is outside and slightly elevated. The more time you spend seeing your world from this bird's-eye view, the faster you will attain your goals—and the more time you will have to spend on that outside-and-slightly-elevated perch. If you are not at the head of your organization, no problem; the systems perspective will quickly propel you upward through the ranks.

It really is this simple: Avoid becoming caught up in the work. Instead, step outside, look down, and isolate individual systems on paper in a 1-2-3 format. Then, deciding overall what you want the systems to accomplish, identify defects as well as outside changing situations. Then improve the systems, always documenting those improvements. Because you have designed these systems to operate without your constant involvement, you can then back off and occasionally (but routinely) monitor and direct things.

I approach all my personal systems from the project engineer's viewpoint: systems to stay fit, keep in touch with extended family, invest money, maintain computers, and even climbing mountains. An especially satisfying one is the daily half hour I spend at home working my "reorganizing system." This is perhaps my simplest system, nothing more than an allocated daily time period dedicated to a narrow purpose: thirty minutes spent reorganizing. It's free-form time used to clean things up, to straighten things out in my office, in my closet, in the garage. Sometimes it's going outside and pruning the shrubs. It's about putting things in order in my life, and it is an antidote to insidious, looming clutter, both physical and mental.

In the beginning of my new systems-oriented lifestyle, I would constantly visualize my personal electric system analogy and its dictate that I be a project engineer. Now I don't think about it too often because the system's mind-set is visceral, hardwired inside my being.

So the analogy you choose matters. Match your world to your analogy, and your everyday actions will become efficient and productive. Not too far down the line, bit-by-bit, freedom and power will materialize.

 ## Toilet Paper

This illustration borders on the nonsensical, but it makes two points. First, that the systems perspective is not common, and second, that the perspective will become permanently ingrained once the logic of it is understood.

As an example of systems thinking, and at the risk of using an awful pun, reaching for a piece of toilet paper is the bottom line. Toilet paper is a mandatory accessory. It may be the one thing that all of us have used daily for all our lives. As an illustration of a system that is ubiquitous, it's perfect.

The act of loading toilet paper on a toilet paper dispenser is a system—a system that proceeds in a linear fashion until the goal is accomplished.

Step one: In the bathroom, approach the sink. Step two: Open the cabinet door underneath the sink. Step three: Reach into the cabinet and grasp a roll of toilet paper. Step four: Take the protective wrapper off the roll. Step five: Approach the toilet paper dispenser with the roll, etc.

Ask yourself the following question. Right now, in your own house or apartment, is the paper roll loaded on the dispenser with the free end of the paper off the top of the roll where it can be easily grasped? Or is the leading edge off the bottom of the roll, against the wall, where one must awkwardly reach underneath the roll to retrieve it?

For the fun of it, over the years I've kept an informal tally. Not counting hotels and motels where professional housecleaners have been instructed on the most efficient positioning, it is a nearly 50-50 split with a slight advantage going to those who chose "top." This means most people don't think one way or the other about the insertion of the roll in the dispenser. (Or, implausibly, one-half the population is adamant that the roll be inserted one way and the other half of the population the other way.)

Not many people think of this triviality. Is it important? Of course not—but that is not what matters here. The important point is that it illustrates the lack of innate systems thinking by the vast majority of people.

Since having the retrieving end of the paper on the top of the roll makes grasping the paper easier, why doesn't everyone load the paper that way every time? Is the task of inserting the roll one way more difficult than inserting it the other way? Not at all. But deciding to always do it this way would require a one-time analysis of the goal and the process—in this case just a few seconds of time—and many of us don't spend time considering underlying processes, even ones so innocuous as this one.

Yes, this is a silly illustration, but try to get past that. See that in considering loading the paper in a different way, you are putting yourself outside and above the act of loading toilet paper. You are deliberately managing the process in order to produce an incrementally better result every single time the process executes in the future.

There is another, more visceral lesson here, and maybe it's a bit unnerving. Because you have considered this toilet paper question, it may cause you to choose to load your rolls in a more deliberate way, or the contrarian in you may consciously decide not to. Whatever your choice, my prediction is that from now on you will think about the process every time you replace a toilet paper roll. Like it or not, due to this end-of-chapter illustration, there is a small slice of systems methodology that has been permanently embedded in your thinking process.

Welcome to my world.

For the record, when I polled my management staff in a staff meeting on how they load their toilet paper at home, I got this response from every single one of them: "Pleeeze! Off the top, of course!" Even in the most mundane tasks, the Centratel staff reflexively take a posture of being outside and slightly elevated. Because they have studied and worked with the logic of systems methodology, it's ingrained permanently.

The *Work the System* mind-set will keep you ever alert to small system improvements that can easily be implemented.

What systems can you see in order to make them better?

CHAPTER 10

Your Strategic Objective and General Operating Principles

I don't want to be a product of my environment. I want my environment to be a product of me.

—FRANK COSTELLO (JACK NICHOLSON)
FROM THE MOVIE *THE DEPARTED* (WARNER BROS., 2006)

To REVIEW: The systems insight arrived because I was under enormous mental and physical pressure. Until that late-night revelation, my strategy was to approach life with a bulldog, damn-the-torpedoes, pound-the-moles, I'm-so-damn-clever persona. It was a toxic brew of arrogance and ignorance—perhaps the most noxious combination of negative human traits. The seething chaos had reared up and was about to crush me for good. Instead, with a flash of insight, it released me. I dropped the bulldog routine, adopted a new outside-and-slightly-elevated perspective, and found new confidence. I knew exactly what moves to make and charged out of my self-imposed prison.

The cure to workplace chaos is to get things down on paper. First, put together the Strategic Objective. It will require a few hours to develop a draft, and a few more hours over another couple of days to get it right. Creating it is pretty much a one-time event, but allow for minor future revisions as the environment changes.

Next, after you write the Strategic Objective's first draft, you will begin work on the General Operating Principles, the contents of which will be accumulated bit-by-bit and then perfected over a few weeks' time.

Still, the total time invested isn't much. Once completed, this document will also remain relatively static over the years.

Third, for your business or your job, you will create a collection of Working Procedures. A Working Procedure is in itself the archetypical system. Products of system improvement, each is an exact guideline for executing the process it describes. (This third form of documentation will be addressed in detail in its own separate chapter.)

Over the long term, you and your staff will spend the majority of documentation time creating new Working Procedures and tweaking existing ones. Although the Strategic Objective and the General Operating Principles will get little mechanical adjustment later on, their fundamentals are key to the creation of your Working Procedures (or, in your personal life, in just navigating the day). In any case, at work, all three documents will remain front and center in your mind.

For every unit of effort and time you expend on the three documents, the return in personal time and financial freedom will be at least hundredfold. *I am not exaggerating.*

CREATING THE STRATEGIC OBJECTIVE

When I bought the ailing Girl Friday Telephone Answering Service in 1984, my goal had been to make the company the best in the industry. That mission quickly evaporated as my staff of seven and I coped with serial fire-killing. For fifteen years we thrashed. But in year sixteen, as we began to plow through the systemizing process and witnessed immediate quality improvement, our goal of being the "Best in the United States" came out from its hiding place and took center stage. We would not just survive: Per verifiable statistics, we would become the best among the more than two thousand competitors in our industry.

The successful leader's job is to keep the wheels of the mechanism turning at full speed, and with enormous efficiency.

As I saw the business for the first time from my new, outside vantage point, I questioned whether Centratel had objectives and a plan for reaching them. I dug in and laid out our goals and strategy in a pragmatic, one-page written document.

The Strategic Objective is the first and most important of the three documents we use to manage Centratel. It gives us direction and prevents us from flailing away in different directions. It is also the foundation for the General Operating Principles and Working Procedures documents, so it *must* come first.

With the Strategic Objective at the forefront, no longer do we squander time and energy heading down roads that don't contribute to the overall objectives of the business.

For Centratel, the ultimate purpose of the Strategic Objective is straightforward, as noted in the use of the present tense in the first line: "We are the highest-quality telephone answering service in the United States." (See appendix B for the complete text of Centratel's Strategic Objective.)

All decisions, large and small, follow from that statement. Every ounce of energy is focused on the primary goal. The Strategic Objective is not a feel-good mission statement based on self-aggrandized hope; it's not something designed to make the board of directors feel good about themselves or intended to impress stockholders and staff. Instead, it's a concise blueprint in which we acknowledge the day-to-day real world in a mechanized, non–wishful thinking way. Without syrupy excess, it includes a brief narration of what the company does, where things are headed, and how management and staff will get there. (The interesting thing is that most business owners already know *what* they have to do to succeed, but because they have hamstrung themselves with fire-killing, they don't have time to even think about establishing goals or developing strategy—*they don't know where to begin.*)

If you can garner the self-discipline to create your Strategic Objective, you will find new strength as you hold the single sheet in your hand. You have direction! And once you have the potent, tangible representation of who you are, where you are going, and how you will get there, you will find it uncanny how the physical world will align itself with what you have written. When you get past the words in this book and take mechanical, physical steps in your real world—the first of which is the creation of your Strategic Objective—you will see for yourself.

Should you create a separate written Strategic Objective for your life? Yes.

CREATING THE GENERAL OPERATING PRINCIPLES

After I completed the first draft of the Strategic Objective, I began creating the second critical document, the General Operating Principles. Congruent with the spirit and the specifics of the Strategic Objective, this became a collection of foundational guidelines for making decisions. In the end, it included thirty separate operating principles, so we called it simply, "30 Principles." You will have your own set of guiding principles, and of course, they may number more or fewer than thirty.

Centratel's 30 Principles document is, of course, a system in itself. (Note that it is a nonlinear system—a set of parameters that are not necessarily directly related, but each of which must be considered across a wide spectrum of decision-making possibilities.) The 30 Principles are tried-and-true, sensible, and simple to understand and remember. They are not flashy. Most of the principles lie quietly underneath the things we do every day. They change very little with evolving circumstances. Over time, they have been tweaked, but their overall immutability is evidence of their soundness.

Think of your General Operating Principles as the guidelines for decision making for your business or your job. It's helpful to make up a set for your personal life, too. You will find your personal principles resemble the set you put together for your work because they reflect your character and your preferred way of approaching the workings of the world. Professional or personal, these principles will remain constant in all aspects of your life.

For an illustration of how the principles can work, consider the following from Centratel's Principle #8: ". . . just a few services implemented in superb fashion." Seven years ago, this tenet mandated that we stop selling cellular telephones as an add-on service. Because we could not depend on the quality of customer service provided by the cellular company for which we were a reseller, this decision gave us better control, and ensured that *all* of our products are high quality. It also simplifies things. Had we not written down this principle in tangible form and then abided by it, we would still be selling cellular phones at a considerable detriment to our overall operation.

Without exception, the businesses that are large and successful are "working their systems." And the ones without structured, sensible protocols and logical direction—most small businesses— are struggling. Very simple.

The General Operating Principles tenets, like the elements of the Strategic Objective, keep us moving in a focused direction whether there's a tendency toward nonaction on the one hand, or a momentary burst of impetuousness on the other. We are dogmatic about following our principles. As with the Strategic Objective, all individual and corporate decisions are focused on the 30 Principles.

Another example is Principle #30: "We strive for a social climate that is serious and quiet yet pleasant, serene, light, and friendly." Because of this principle, our office *is* like that: the principle is a hoop through which all decisions must pass. The live decorative plants, the special lighting, the physical layout of the office, the clear-cut policies and guidelines, and the like make Centratel an attractive place to work.

Don't expect your principles document to be finished in one sitting. Because it was sometimes two minutes here and five minutes there, it took me more than a month to create the rough list, select the proper wording, and polish it. Begin by writing down several principles you already have in mind. Then take notes as additional principles pop into your head. Be sure to seek others' input as you put your list together. (Centratel's 30 Principles are listed in appendix C.)

Why Can't We Find Employees?

It's our greatest challenge: Centratel's pay and benefits are very good, but no matter how aggressively we advertise our positions, we don't have many job applicants. Because we have a hard time finding qualified people, we are fortunate our current staff see little turnover. But the irony of simultaneous recruitment challenges and staff stability is understandable. If one digs a bit, it becomes clear why we have problems finding job applicants—and the good fortune of having high staff stability. It's our drug-testing policy.

Before we instituted drug testing, we had plenty of job applicants, but there was also high staff turnover. A staff that uses drugs is flighty, and a flighty staff means call-handling expertise achieved through long-term experience won't happen.

Our brutal judgment is that only a limited number of service-industry job candidates are drug free. It's a painful, almost unbelievable conclusion, but we operate on that basis because the statistics bear it out. The choice seems to be, "I'd rather smoke dope and earn minimum wage with no benefits at a menial job, then *not* smoke dope at Centratel, where I could earn more than double minimum wage with full benefits." Ouch.

Many business owners understand the truth of this so they don't invoke drug testing. Of those who do, it's a gamble. I know of one local restaurant that had to close its doors after an impromptu drug screening of all its employees. They had to terminate employment for nine of their twelve people. Another local business, a new, huge "box" store, selected twenty people for its automotive department. Sixteen of the twenty failed the drug testing.

Did our decision to use drug screening stem from an outside-and-slightly-elevated perspective? There is no question. Per our Strategic Objective, we looked down on our business and decided we required a stable workforce. We decided to trade the chaos of high staff turnover for the staid challenge of finding drug-free people who are steady, superb performers.

To be sure, the introduction of a drug-testing policy must be handled with care, supported by a well-thought-out written policy.

Do you see recurring negative situations with the people in your workplace where clarification on paper would eliminate future contention? Is there a mechanical filter that might clarify things?

CHAPTER 11

Your Working Procedures

Keep your eyes on the road, your hands upon the wheel . . .

—From the song "Roadhouse Blues,"

written and performed by The Doors (Elektra/Asylum, 1970)

THE EXECUTION OF A RECURRING PROTOCOL varies with the time of day, the weather, or the mood not only among the individuals performing the process but also for any one person. In the workplace, the challenge and the solution is to make these ubiquitous organic human processes as solid and reliable as the mechanical objects that surround us. Boring but true, we do this with documentation.

At Centratel, we analyze a system individually, document it as it is, find the cause of any recurring problem or inefficiency, devise a system improvement to fix the problem or cure the inefficiency, and then create a prototype written Working Procedure. We then test the procedure in the real world, tweaking it into a final form that precisely explains the desired execution of the process. The new Working Procedure is released, and the Centratel staff follow it exactly as written. That's it!

A system improvement requires a written Working Procedure. The Working Procedure makes the system tangible—something to be seen, grasped, understood, perfected, shared, and then applied exactly the same way every time. Know this: A this-will-happen-every-single-time protocol won't materialize via mind reading, a one-time conversation, or when it is discussed in a meeting.

> An effective process *must* be set in concrete, and that means creating it in hard and/or soft copy, distributing it, and then ensuring that it is implemented.

You who are managers must consider it your ethical responsibility—not just an efficient way to operate—to provide working procedures for your staff. I occasionally remind my employees that it is my personal obligation to provide them with the tools to do their jobs. Expecting an employee to be able to read the boss's mind is not just an absurd expectation, it's unfair. I tell them that.

CREATING WORKING PROCEDURES

At Centratel, the same inefficiencies kept cropping up over and over, devouring any bottom-line profit and literally killing me physically. These recurring problems were the natural result of undocumented, uncontrolled processes. Now Working Procedures, products of the system-improvement process, prevent these serial headaches by providing exact direction for flawless operation.

We break things down into small "system package units" by extracting systems from the daily operation and then outlining them on paper in a simple linear, chronological format. (First, this happens; second, that happens; third, ... etc.) We also have a number of nonlinear Working Procedures that are better explained in either a narrative or a bullet-point format.

After documenting a given protocol as it is, we analyze the mechanical process, and from that, develop a streamlined finished product with attending final documentation.

Then we implement it. Everyone follows the new procedure exactly as it is written. Over time, we tweak it to perfection.

We follow this system-improvement routine over and over again, making every individual system perfect.

The finished products are our "Working Procedures," or simply, "Procedures." At Centratel, we have approximately three hundred of them. Depending on the task, they can range from the utter simplicity of two short sentences to line after line of detail encompassing half a dozen pages.

Feathers in the Wind

Remember that a set of instructions for a process is not a Working Procedure until it is written down. Instructions that are not written down are feathers in the wind. Think of it this way: You can't represent yourself as being a college graduate unless you have the diploma in hand. No diploma, no degree. No exceptions. You are either a college graduate or you are not. Think of your Working Procedures in the same way: If they are not tangible, they don't exist.

THREE KEY POINTS IN CREATING WORKING PROCEDURES

Key point number one for designing, producing, and executing procedures is to use the "best solution" for a recurring problem or process every single time the problem or process surfaces. At Centratel, we collectively decide what works best in the majority of circumstances; we "cast the procedure in concrete" in written form; then we apply the procedure exactly as written every single time. No matter who applies the protocol, the same "best solution" will always be applied, and therefore, "best results" will almost always occur.

Will the Working Procedure provide the perfect solution for every situation? No, but it will be perfect *most* of the time, and that is far better than haphazard solutions that are applied on a whim. So over time, incremental "best results" add up to a "big best result" for the primary system.

Key point number two is that procedure documentation is not limited to just the obvious problem areas. It applies to all internal processes. Documenting a seemingly flawless process will often reveal small imperfections. It will take a while to turn every process into a Working Procedure, but the efficiency increases earned from this effort will accumulate. If a subsystem is already 90 percent effective, yet it can be boosted to a level of 98 percent effectiveness, that's a good thing. What could be better for a primary system than to spend time improving all of its subsystems?

Key point number three is to create your Working Procedure documents for anyone "off-the-street." This means that someone who doesn't even work for your organization could perform the process. More on this later.

These days, little goes wrong at Centratel, and the things that do go wrong are fixed immediately. As fire-killing is reduced and more and more processes are automated and delegated, more free time becomes available. This is the main reason our managers seldom work more than forty hours a week and why my workweek, as company CEO and general manager, is rarely more than two hours. This overall efficiency is also the reason I now earn far more in a month than what I used to earn in a year.

OUR FIRST WORKING PROCEDURE

Coming immediately after my midnight epiphany, our first Working Procedure was the "Deposit Procedure," which provided our management staff with exact directions for processing the dozens of client payments that come in the mail each day. This process involves more than the actual bank deposit. It also includes receiving incoming checks, crediting them to clients' accounts in the receivables software, and cross-checking totals. Nine years ago, when we created this first Working Procedure, three management people, including me, were authorized to make a deposit. No written instructions existed.

The reason we focused on the Deposit Procedure first was because it was a critical system and it had deep flaws. It seemed to be our most troublesome process. Without any set-in-writing protocol, and with each of us performing the task in our own unique way, we too often made random mistakes, seldom in Centratel's favor (and if they *were* in our favor, a client was shortchanged). Sometimes we applied payments to the wrong accounts, and too many times deposit sums were incorrect. One time, a $3,000 deposit was lost by one of our managers, only to be inadvertently found weeks later under her car seat. Of course, any wasted money was subtracted dollar-for-dollar from the bottom line. As we describe in Operating Principle #10, "The money we save or waste is *not* Monopoly money!"

And with all the gyrations and outright errors, the process was taking far too much time and *that* was a waste. So the three of us put our heads together. After thoroughly interviewing my managers, this first system improvement/Working Procedure took me four hours to compose. Then, to tweak it to perfection, it took maybe three more hours spread over a couple more days.

This first Deposit Procedure contained *fifty-three* individual steps. Here is how they went:

Step 1: Put the envelopes in a stack in front of you on the desk and open all the envelopes. (Do not take the contents out of the envelopes.)

Step 2: Open the receivables software and go to the deposit module.

Step 3, etc., proceeded through all the paper processing, until Step 50, which is take the deposit to the bank and make the deposit.

Step 51: At the bank, get a deposit slip and check the amount deposited to make sure it matches the amount on the deposit slip.

Step 52: Back in the office, staple the bank deposit slip to the upper left-hand corner of the receivables batch printout.

Step 53: Place the printout in the daily deposit file in the receivables file cabinet in the CFO's office.

We agreed that if any one of us saw room for improvement in the procedure, we would collaborate on the spot. If we all agreed the change would be good, we would instantly update the procedure's documentation—and just as quickly implement the revised procedure.

This is important: A published procedure itself is inflexible, yet we will immediately change the construction of the procedure if the change will improve it. (This "change it immediately" parameter was per our do-it-now Operating Principle #14.)

We put the Deposit Procedure into play. From then on, no matter who performed it, the deposit process proceeded the same way every single time. Over time, we tweaked it even more and each time we did, the procedure got better. We built double-checks into it so we knew for certain that the payments were tallied correctly, and we built in steps to ensure that the deposits made it to the bank.

Because we put the procedure together in a simple 1-2-3-step off-the-street format, anyone within the company could make a deposit. As a result, I didn't make deposits anymore; we delegated my portion of the task to another staff member (and because of the written procedure's simplicity, I didn't have to take the time to train someone else to do the task). Completing that first Working Procedure reduced my personal workload by at least a couple of hours each week. That's two hours per week over nine years. Do the math.

In its own way, that first procedure was a tiny masterpiece, and yet we continued to polish it to even more effectiveness. Since we started using it, there has been only one small, easily corrected error. Of course, repairing that particular error meant yet another small improvement in the written procedure (per General Operating Principle #7). Today, the Deposit Procedure is down to merely twenty-three steps because of better software and my staff's learned ability to simplify, streamline, and economize. Per William of Ockham, simplicity is indeed evidence a solution is sound.

Even though we put the first procedure together so long ago, I remember this vividly: It was satisfying beyond words to know the deposit processing was finally stable and efficient. And it was no small satisfaction to realize I would never have to personally handle another deposit.

The Working Procedure, a mandatory element of the system-improvement process, is not theory or feel-good fluff. Rather, it is something that is down-and-dirty *useful* in the real-time world. It reminds me of the title of a short story by Raymond Carver: "A Small, Good Thing." That's what a Working Procedure is. A small, good thing. The idea is to make your business and your life a huge accumulation of small, good things.

The Test of Time

Regarding the Strategic Objective and the Operating Principles, know that an endorsement of their viability is the test of time. If you are truly using them and they change little over the months and years, this is confirmation they are sound. On the other hand, Working Procedures should constantly evolve, and that evolution is confirmation *they* are valid.

A WORK IN PROGRESS

What was our second Working Procedure? We analyzed, dissected, and set in stone the methodology the telephone service representatives (TSRs) use to process incoming calls.

Our TSRs have executed this Working Procedure thousands of times *every day* since we put it into place so long ago. Precisely following this procedure is the ticket to relaxing and enjoying their work. For example, if there is an error in delivering a message, the TSR holds no blame as long as he or she followed the message delivery procedure exactly. As it turns out, nearly all message relay problems are due to system error, not TSR error. Because our TSRs follow written procedures exactly, nearly all errors are traced back to clients who have not informed us of changes—changes that invalidate the previous, on-record Working Procedure for that client. The procedure was at fault, not the employee. The cure is to make an immediate mechanical update in that client's Message-Relay Working Procedure, not chew someone out. This lack of finger-pointing contributes much to the serenity of the office.

In the months after we instituted the Deposit and TSR Answering Procedures, we analyzed and streamlined scores of other recurring processes, including how to put together the staffing schedule, how to streamline collections, and how to pay the bills. We created procedures for performing the monthly customer invoicing, ensuring various housekeeping tasks were done on a regular basis, making the most effective sales presentations, and so forth.

For some undocumented processes that were in place, our system-improvement analysis suggested that creating a Working Procedure wasn't necessary, and in fact we had been wasting our time performing the process at all! Discarding paper records of customer contacts is a good example of this purging action. In analyzing the process, we discovered that after years of accumulating hard-copy evidence of every client inter-action, no staff member had *ever* gone back to those files for information!

When these obsolete processes occasionally appeared, we dumped them with a flourish, a collective grin on our faces. For other less-than-efficient tasks, we found ourselves devising radically altered protocols, with final versions unrecognizable from the originals. It was a cleansing process. The assertive effort to root out and improve every single system led us to these unexpected deletions and substitutions.

Centratel was becoming dramatically more efficient. We worked hard, improving and documenting system after system. Interestingly, there were rarely relationships among the procedures we created or revised. The sore spots we tackled were unrelated, but we had a methodology for setting priorities: We straightened out the weightiest problems first.

As we worked up the new procedures and "released" them as official, I found myself delegating more and more tasks that had been my responsi-bility. I simply handed a completed Working Procedure over to the appro-priate manager and walked away. I was steadily gaining additional personal time to reinvest in tackling more problem areas. It was the same situation for my managers as they delegated processes down the chain of command, while the rate of incoming problems continued to decrease.

Although the original, one-time heavy lifting—the documentation of all of our procedures in one gigantic effort—ended years ago, we continue to apply the system-improvement methodology on a moment-to-moment basis. No longer do we fire-kill. Instead, we work our systems.

JUST WRITE IT DOWN

At first, it will seem like you don't have the spare time to work through the system-improvement/Working Procedures process. That's a mistaken premise because if you think creating procedures is a spare time task, the process will take a backseat to the crisis du jour. Procedure documentation must go to the top of your priority list or the process won't start, or it will be derailed in a week or two. You will fail. For your business or job, raise the importance level of writing procedures to the number one position, even above some of the fire-killing of the day. Forget about "finding spare time" to do this work. Don't waste your efforts by starting on that premise; *there is no such thing as "spare" time.*

Although it might take an hour or two a day to write up and then institute a new procedure—do it. Personal-time savings will begin immediately upon implementation. Soon you will crave spending time on your quest to document your entire operation, while the time you spend doing nonprocedures documentation will be frustrating.

Remember, the litmus test for simplicity is that anyone from outside the company, "off the street," could perform the procedure. Of course, depending on your business or job, this simplicity might have to be more specific. For example, writing an electrical engineering procedure for an "off-the-street layperson" is not going to work. But writing an electrical engineering procedure for an "off-the-street electrical engineer" is reasonable.

With Working Procedures, you will save enormous time in training people to full effectiveness. An employee who doesn't know the ropes of a particular task will simply read the procedure and then get the job done without assistance from other staff members. There will be no error-prone and belabored "learning by osmosis." (Note that first-timers are the best source for tweaking a procedure to perfection. Have them review the procedure, and then ask them what can be improved to make it truly off-the-street. Someone using the procedure for the first time has fresh eyes and is not jaded by an insider's can't-see-the-forest-for–the-trees limited vision.)

And of course, for yourself and for your managers, the extra time saved is used for improving the systemization even more: the "cycle of increasing returns."

Here's another large plus: With written Working Procedures in place, your operation will become more professional. Your people will recognize this and raise their expectations for themselves and for their company. Your staff's pride and enthusiasm will shine brightly for your customers.

A MACHINE TO IMPLEMENT TASKS

Our point-of-sale internal communications hinge on Microsoft Outlook, which keeps us organized through its standard calendar, task list, and contact information sections. For a manager, the most important part of the software is the tasking feature. In a moment's notice the leader can issue instructions to a staff member that include precise directions as to what must be accomplished, as well as a date by which the task must be completed. The job doesn't disappear from the staff member's and manager's task lists until the job is finished. In the process of job completion, Outlook prompts the staff member to provide regular updates. The task won't fall through the cracks, and no error of omission will occur.

We use this same system to automatically ensure recurring working procedures are completed on time and without fail. And the feature is also perfect for keeping track of personal tasks.

There are other mechanical methodologies, such as day planners and wall-mounted task-list bulletin boards, but computer-based ones are superior because they are fast and easily shared and in your face. Research the numerous computer-based organizers that are available, or create your own.

A PROCEDURE TO CREATE PROCEDURES

As we first began creating Working Procedures at Centratel, I felt compelled to do much of the documentation myself. It took me months to see that this was unnecessary, and I caution you not to fall into the same trap.

There is a system for everything, so certainly there is one that will oversee the creation of procedures by people other than you—a "Procedure for Procedures." This master document lays out the format and tone you want staff to use in creating everyday Working Procedures. Once complete, you will train your managers to use it exactly. (Centratel's Procedure for Procedures is listed in appendix D.)

The core of the training is the Procedure for Procedures itself. And when I say train, I mean *train*. Each manager must "get it." Set aside group classes that will be uninterrupted. You will be the teacher, and your managers will be the students. Consider having your staff study this book. (Note: A quiz for testing comprehension of the fundamental *Work the System* principles is available at workthesystem.com/quiz.)

An added benefit of having your staff create Working Procedures is that the process will encourage them to buy into the methodology. They will see the beauty of it firsthand, from the bottom up. Be ruthless, however, in examining the procedures they create. You want to know what's happening.

It is the leader's job to make sure staff members have exact guidelines for each task they do. Then, it is the employee's job to follow the instructions precisely.

On this point I am adamant: It is the staff member's first responsibility to implement a procedure *exactly* as written. There is no latitude here. There must be strict adherence. Do my staff members comply? Yes, for four reasons: First, simple logic. Because the written procedure methodology works, they buy into it 100 percent. Second, as mentioned, they are involved with the creation and the approval of nearly all procedures, so they are fully vested in them. (In fact, Centratel's staff write 98 percent of all procedures and have a heavy hand in the other 2 percent that I personally create.) Third, if an employee has a good idea for improving a procedure, we will make an instant modification—with no bureaucratic hang-ups. No one wades through the system-improvement/Working Procedure process grumbling about how intractable it is. Fourth, if a procedure is followed and something goes wrong, the staff member is not at fault. It is the procedure that is in error.

Ruthlessness and Flexibility

Point number three in the previous paragraph merits repeating. Yes, be ruthless in insisting that your staff follow procedures exactly, but balance this strict rule with the understanding that if a procedure must be changed in order to remain effective, with proper consensus it will be changed instantly. The procedure itself is rock solid and inflexible until the moment your management staff agree that changes are necessary. At Centratel, we make the decision to modify a procedure *right now*, in an ad hoc meeting any time, any place. We modify the procedure in that moment, and in the next moment the adjusted procedure will be distributed to all parties affected. Unwieldy bureaucracy is the enemy, and each time one of us witnesses slow-moving decision making in other businesses, it confirms for us that our own operation is flexible, efficient, and potent.

The perfect example of bureaucratic paralysis is, of course, government—the quintessential nonprofit organization that is in business to spend other people's money. Government has given written procedures a bad name. If there is a ubiquitous generalization about "the nightmare of paperwork and bureaucracy," one can say thank you to the overabundance of governmental organizations that surround and engulf us.

Your Competitors Don't Do This

I used to be involved with answering-service trade groups. I've served as president of two national associations and was a board member for a couple of others. I became knowledgeable about the politics of my industry and enjoyed communicating with my peers.

At the tail end of my involvement with these groups, I gave a presentation to sixty answering-service owners in Las Vegas. The topic was "Procedures and Their Importance." At the beginning of the one-hour session, I asked the group, "How many of you have written procedures for your operation?" *No one raised a hand!* I am still shocked to think of that day, but nonetheless, operating without written guidelines is the way it is for most small businesses.

A majority of small-business owners are looking for answers in the wrong places because they have not gone through the dissection process that thorough documentation demands. They don't have goals, and they don't see the internal inefficiencies of their systems, so they seek spur-of-the-moment "global" solutions: some quick fix—a magic pill—that in one fell swoop will make everything better. Often, the magic pill they seek is a godlike new employee, a mind reader and fortune-teller, an extraordinary individual who will flawlessly manage the business and, with little guidance, take it to its deserved success. Of course, in the real world, these people don't exist.

Here is the curious fact that most small-business owners/managers don't get: Terrific employees *are* out there, but in a non-documented business, none will function anywhere near their potential because mind reading and fortune-telling are not things humans can do, no matter how advanced their IQ or educational pedigree. (See appendix A for an article I wrote regarding documentation and employees.)

At the risk of appearing impudent, I ask, is it any wonder that Centratel operates and advertises itself as the highest-quality telephone answering service in the United States? My staff know exactly what to do and exactly how to do it. Errors seldom occur because actions are the most efficient possible, based on the staff relentlessly tweaking systems to perfection. And when there is an error, that error spurs us to devise an even better mechanical system for the future. We don't spend our time coping with bad results that are the products of neglected systems. We work our systems so that bad results don't happen!

It's elementary: *If each component of an organization is nearly flawless, the organization as a whole will be nearly flawless,* as evidenced by profitability, net worth, customer-reported–error rate, client longevity, staff longevity, reputation, etc.

Centratel's five managers are tenacious in applying the *Work the System* strategy. They assertively search for system inefficiencies, revel in devising system improvements, and enthusiastically create Working Procedures to make those systems permanently efficient. Their individual reward includes reasonable-length workweeks, personal freedom with lots of room for creativity, and intense pride in what they do and where they work. Also, they are highly paid.

Systems, systems, systems!

It all adds up to supreme satisfaction for the staff, superb quality for customers, and solid profits for my partner and me. Further tangible evidence of our efficiency: In our TSR quality statistics for the twelve months prior to the publication of this book, we averaged one client-reported error for every 9,990 messages processed. (In that time period, one TSR, Kathleen, had but a single error in the more than 60,000 messages she personally processed!)

Our service rates? They are higher than the competition's—but not by much—because our systems methodology has, while creating unmatched quality, eliminated waste and generated tremendous cost-savings efficiency. Our customers? Successful in their own businesses, they are happy with the arrangement with Centratel as illustrated by our average client tenure, which exceeds seven years (remember, the average new business has an 80 percent chance of failing in the first five years).

How about your small business, or you and your position in the company where you work? Attain the systems-perspective epiphany and then buckle down to start the documentation. The day you begin, you will be in select company, way out in front of 98 percent of your small-business competitors (or, if you work for someone else, your coworkers).

Note that written Working Procedures are not necessary for your personal life. Why? First (and forgive my firm grasp of the obvious), it's just silly to write down how you will maintain the car, work on the details of your marriage, stay in shape, pay bills, or develop a system for staying in touch with friends. With your new vision ingrained, you'll handle these processes systematically without having to write up documentation.

Second, a primary reason for creating Working Procedures is to make sure that the people you supervise are handling details just as you would handle them. Since *you* are the only one operating your personal life, it is good enough to hardwire your personal Working Procedures in your head without documentation. The exceptions? Lists for travel or shopping, travel itineraries, to-do lists, and intricate technical instructions.

A Summary of Procedure Documentation

1. At work, every recurring process requires a Working Procedure. The procedure will precisely define the best method of performing the action, handling the situation, or answering the question.

2. A problem is a good thing when your staff takes it as a cue for the creation or modification of a Working Procedure. However, be reasonable. Do not create an unwieldy bureaucracy by writing up procedures for problems that are random or

seldom—in other words, problems that have little chance of resurfacing. There is a danger of being inundated with a massive conglomeration of rarely used procedures, thus creating complexity due to the sheer volume of information. Solving infrequent problems requires just a bit of common sense based on the guidelines provided by the Strategic Objective and General Operating Principles documents.

3. Be sure your staff are involved in creating the new procedures. In fact, relentlessly delegate.

4. By making procedures identical in presentation, their individual instructions will come through loud and clear without becoming confused by various style or tone variations. This is where you as the leader come in. It's up to you to keep things on track.

5. Without exception, test every new procedure. Before releasing, give it to a staff member who will carefully go through the steps to spot glitches. Take this stance: In a new or revamped procedure, glitches will *always* occur.

6. As the leader, sign off on procedures yourself. Make sure they are consistent with your overall vision. Keep things in order and always in line with your Strategic Objective and Operating Principles. That's your job.

Note: The documentation process can be made simple and fast with *Work the System Easy Template Software*™. Go to workthesystem.com/easy for information. Also, the entire *Work the System* process is presented in a two-day "Boot Camp" in Bend, Oregon. Go to workthesystem.com/bootcamp for details.

Frank Zappa's System-Improvement Strategy

If you think your business or work situation is "different" and therefore some of these principles won't necessarily apply, consider this: Frank Zappa (1940–1993) was one of the most brilliant avant-garde rock artists of the

'70s and '80s. He scored each note of every song and required 100 percent performance accuracy from his band members. After a concert, when most of his contemporaries would likely be attending a post-performance party, Frank would be conducting a mandatory-attendance postmortem with his backup band.

During these performance autopsies, individual players were assessed a $50 fine for each and every note missed. New band members were quick to challenge Zappa's recollection of the score and their individual performances; more-experienced members knew better. Frank's perfect recall of the performance was easy enough to verify: The evening's audio recordings would confirm what Frank already knew, and the fines would stand. Band members who were fined were not likely to forget to rehearse their parts before the next performance. Frank set the bar high and his success is rock music history.

Does this attention to detail seem persnickety? Your challenge is to embrace this level of attention rather than be repelled by it. The end result? Less work. More time. More money.

By the way, Frank Zappa never used drugs and was quite the family man.

Are there processes at your workplace that yield different results every time, depending on who performs the process? If statistics are gathered for any given process, are there exact written instructions for how to gather and analyze them? As the leader of your organization, to what level of strictness do you hold your staff members accountable? Do they know what to expect?

PART THREE

FURTHER CONSIDERATIONS

CHAPTER 12
Good Enough

A good plan violently executed right now is far better
than a perfect plan executed next week.

—GEORGE S. PATTON

To PREFACE THIS DISCUSSION, understand this is about *work*, not about relaxing or some combination of the two. If you own a business, your mission is to work hard but not long, to reduce the workweek significantly, and to make more money than you require. If you have a job, the goal is to use your forty-hour workweek to produce large quantities of superior output in order to quickly ascend the management ranks so you are earning serious money and can call your own shots.

This needs to be said and it's a good time to say it: No matter what your situation, if you are going to work, then work! Turn the radio off, get your feet off the desk, stop the pointless babbling with coworkers, and put your head down. *Get in, do the work, and get out.*

Smell the flowers later when it's time to give those flowers all your attention. Combining working and relaxing will result in frustration in both areas: in your work, long hours spent in a mishmash of unsatisfying mediocrity, and in your leisure, an unsettled persona.

LESS-THAN-PERFECT PERFORMANCE IS AN OKAY THING

For the *Work the System* method, here is a qualifier: Getting things too perfect is counterproductive and shortsighted. The following story from my background illustrates the good-enough concept and the reality that better than good enough is usually a waste of time and money.

When I was twenty-four years old, studying land surveying in technical school, our instructor told the class a story at the beginning of the year to prep us for the technical lessons that would follow. The story setting was the early '70s, when the typical survey crew consisted of a party chief, who was responsible for supervising the actual in-the-field survey work, and three additional crew members.

The party chief was given a project, and it was up to him (in those days, it was almost always a "him") to take the crew into the field, do the job, and report back to the owner of the surveying company with accurate and usable notes so a map of the surveyed land could be created. With the notes and the map, the landowner's questions of property size, boundary lines, and future development possibilities could be answered.

A survey project is a linear, encapsulated process—yes, a system—and a project begins when the survey-company owner tells the party chief, in not so many words, "Here's the job. I presume you can handle it. Be quick and accurate according to the specifications I give you, then come back and give me your field notes so the draftsman can make a map of the property. Then I can get paid by the land owner."

BEN AND JOHN

This scenario is about a surveying company and two of the half dozen survey crews it employs. The party chiefs and their respective crews are to survey the boundaries of a landowner's two parcels of land. The owner of the survey firm assigns the first parcel to one crew (with Ben as the party chief), and the second parcel to another crew (with John as the party chief). The owner of the land wants the surveys performed in order to get a general feel for where the property lines and property corners are located.

The survey-company owner provides Ben and John with brief yet detailed verbal instructions about what is required. As in any survey project, the crews must measure the distances and angles of the property boundaries quickly, efficiently, and accurately. The degree of accuracy depends on the reason for the survey, and of course, higher degrees of accuracy require more crew time and therefore are more expensive. In survey work, it's a balancing act between speed and accuracy as the crew moves along, physically marking property corners and providing distance and angle statistics to the party chief, who takes notes.

Time is always of the essence to the survey-company owner because he pays his crews by the hour but receives a flat fee from the client. In this story, time is even more critical because the property owner has a deadline to meet. The crews must get to work immediately and finish the two surveys promptly.

The surveying will be challenging. Each parcel is wooded and undulating, and has irregular perimeters. Each is similar in size—several miles in circumference. Based on the survey-company owner's verbal briefing, each party chief makes a determination of how much accuracy is required to survey his particular parcel.

The next day, the two crews separately gather the necessary materials and equipment and head off to their projects. The two crews go to work, each surveying their respective properties.

Ben decides his survey requires measurement to the nearest one-hundredth of a foot—a high level of accuracy. Using a theodolite (a sophisticated tripod-mounted instrument for measuring precise angles), and a "steel chain" for measuring near-exact distances, his crew slowly and methodically works through their project, carefully marking the physical property corners, exactly measuring distances and angles, checking and double-checking their work. Ben takes careful notes in his field book. The four are focused and fastidious, their work exact.

It takes the crew four days to complete the survey at a total cost of $800 to their boss, the owner of the survey company. Their work is perfect; the submitted survey notes are neat and concise especially because Ben took an additional day to review them.

In the meantime, John determined that his crew would survey their parcel with less accuracy, measuring only to the nearest whole foot and allowing his crew to finish the job quickly. Using the same equipment as Ben's crew, but not taking time to measure distances and angles as precisely, the crew moves at full tilt. They mark approximate property corners while rapidly taking angle and distance measurements, and John takes quick notes, double-checking them as he goes.

They complete the survey in just one day. John immediately submits his work, telling the survey-company owner that the measured distances and angles are not precise. The submitted notes are smudged and wrinkled, evidence of a quick-moving crew that is not overly concerned with appearances. The total cost for John's one-day survey is $200.

The owner of the survey company reviews the notes of each party chief and . . . *fires Ben!*

The party chief who took so much care and produced such accurate work is *fired*? Why?

In land surveyor parlance, Ben committed a "blunder." The survey didn't require measurements to one-hundredth of a foot, so the additional time expended to provide that level of accuracy was an utter waste. In his original briefing to each party chief, the survey-company owner had explained the property owner wanted only a general idea of where the property lines and property corners were located. Ben had not listened carefully, self-enamored with his ability to produce tremendous accuracy. In his zeal for precision, he wasted three days and $600 by providing a huge amount of useless information.

It was a blunder based on arrogance and narrow vision. Precision that is not required is often just that.

98 PERCENT PERFECTION

Time and money wasted is time and money gone forever. And a waste of time and money means some other positive thing that could have happened, didn't.

The "Good Enough" rule is especially applicable to Working Procedures. A 100 percent perfect document that took forever to create carries an unintended imperfection: The extra time spent creating the masterpiece is lost forever, therefore the finished product carries an embedded taint and—catch-22—can never be called "perfect."

So make your procedures detailed but don't make them *too* detailed. They should be good enough so the desired results are consistently produced, and so someone "off the street" can execute them, but no more. See it this way: In putting your procedures together quickly, you are reaching a kind of perfection—the perfection of a useful product created without waste.

Throughout this book I have asserted that you must "tweak your procedures to perfection." Now you better understand why my definition of perfection is 98 percent, not 100 percent.

Regarding the *Work the System* process, are there exceptions to the rule? Yes, there are two. Both your Strategic Objective and General Operating Principles should be as close to 100 percent perfect as possible, despite the additional time it takes to get there. These documents are your guiding lights for today and tomorrow. They are short, and you and your people will read them repeatedly. Imperfections will stand out, overshadowing the message. The Strategic Objective and the Operating Principles documents are the brief summations of everything you are and how you will proceed so, yes, spend good time on them.

Beware Useless Information and Whining

Guard your consciousness and your focus. Don't waste time on useless information or complain about what you can't influence.

With the people and things around you, be militant about relegating unimportant media- and advertisement-driven trivia to the trash pile of useless information that resides on the periphery of your consciousness. Don't let zero-value details poison what is important to your life, no matter how dogged the encroachment.

Do you get caught up with what is not fair in the world? That's an utter waste of time if you can't accomplish something tangible to fix the unfairness (and whining and complaining don't count as accomplishments . . .).

Choose your battles.

This Is Not a (Expletive) Clock

For a while, I was a construction inspector working with power line crews that build overhead transmission lines. Following written construction designs, the crews use massive crane trucks to insert enormous seventy-eighty-foot wood poles in the ground. Then they go back to string heavy-gauge conductor (wire) between them.

The men on these crews are weather-beaten, hard-living, all-American linemen. Good men, straight out of the union hall, they have the surly countenance of loggers and roughnecks and are not apt to "suffer fools gladly."

I was working with such a crew in the hot, windswept backcountry of eastern Oregon when I found fault with the work they had just completed. In sighting down a half-mile-long line stretch of six poles, one pole was clearly two to three feet out of alignment with the others.

I pointed out the problem to the crusty foreman. To correct the error, he would have to order his men to go back with the heavy equipment, remove the poorly placed pole from the ground, fill in the old hole, re-drill a new hole, and then reset the pole in the proper alignment. The foreman was not pleased. Nobody likes to do the same job twice, especially when there is a degree of humiliation attached.

I will never forget his grizzled scowl and clear disdain for college boy inspectors like me as he growled, "We're building a (expletive) power line, not a (expletive) clock!"

Well, the pole *was* out of alignment and his crew did go back to reset it properly, but his power line/clock metaphor has stuck with me through the years. That cut-to-the-bone comment, however off-target in that particular circumstance, is an enduring reminder that the quality of work must not exceed the required result.

Here's a real-world question for you: When you reconcile your personal checkbook, do you reconcile to the nearest cent? Why? Why not reconcile to the nearest dollar? Wouldn't eliminating a lot of minor detail make for a lot less work? Think about other areas in your life where you are manipulating too much information. Are you seeking useless detail?

CHAPTER 13

Errors of Omission

We do not so much look at things as overlook them.

—Zen proverb

It's an interesting exercise to look back and ask, "In descending order of impact, what have been the top five mistakes of my life?" When I propose this question to friends, they chide me about dwelling on the past and focusing on the negative. Yes, I understand all that, but if one spends some time summarizing, an interesting commonality will surface, one that will be useful for future decision making.

It is important to approach the task with an objective and detached persona. Take time to think it out, get it down on paper with objectivity, and the list will stand the test of time. That's how it has been for me; my top-five list has remained unchanged for seventeen years.

In my list—and I'll bet yours, too—the largest errors were not the result of overt mistakes; they were the outcome of failing to take steps that should have been taken. These are "errors of omission." The large errors of omission are bad enough, but the small ones can add up to an equally dire end.

Is there a primary cause for errors of omission? Yes. Too often, it's procrastination, or what I call a lack of "quiet courage." (I discuss quiet courage in the next chapter.)

CHRONIC, COVERT, AND INSIDIOUS

A list of a life's five largest mistakes could include not finishing college, not heeding that stop sign just before the traffic accident, or not starting that savings account way back in the teen years. What about not keeping one's mouth shut at a crucial moment, or not doing the little things that could have saved a marriage? Or maybe declining to apologize when it was the perfect time to do so? Other errors of omission: failing to get enough sleep, forgetting to lock the door of the car, and not submitting taxes by April 15.

"Not taking action" is the physical manifestation of any error of omission.

What Haven't You Done?

The errors-of-omission principle is a simple enough concept, but it lies hidden, buried beneath the jumble of life's demands. As usual, recognition is 90 percent of the solution. And just as the outside-and-slightly-elevated perspective provides a better vantage point for observation of life's hard and cold mechanics, internalizing the errors-of-omission principle gives you a better stance from which to deal with your own natural inclinations.

What follows is a list of still more errors of omission to heed. Think of examples in your own life.

Failure to

- Exercise leads to a lethargic energy level and an unhealthy mind/body.
- Recognize birthdays, anniversaries, and holidays contributes to the transformation of a passionate relationship to one of mutual complacency.
- Pay a bill leads to late charges.
- Get enough sleep leads to a less-than-productive next day.
- Make the phone call, close the sale, smooth out the misunderstanding, or ask for help contributes to less-than-desirable outcomes.
- Clean the house contributes to an underlying sense of confusion.

- Write up a Working Procedure for staff leads to repeated mistakes.
- Apologize or admit a mistake leads to the end of a relationship.
- Create a daily schedule that includes time to build the business or the relationship leads to no change, no improvement, and continued general malaise.

The errors-of-omission principle works hand-in-hand with the axiom "What you say or think is irrelevant; it's what you *do* that counts." Nike's "Just Do It" credo, which is as metaphysical and profound as a maxim can be, is perhaps the most recognizable three-word sequence in the English language, and as such, reconfirms Ockham's admonition for "parsimony in scientific explanation."

Inaction Is Action

In any context, an omission is something left out, something not done. Here's the rub: It is a *choice* not to do something that should be done. So laziness and procrastination are choices. *Not taking action is a choice!* No matter what we do or don't do, we are always making choices.

Sitting on a couch and not moving a muscle is a *choice*. In this life, at a minimum, we take up physical space, absorb resources, and create waste. Even if we do nothing, we continue to have an impact on the world around us. So it makes sense to get off the couch, take that body that is using up space anyway, and do something constructive with it.

It boils down to the usual utter simplicity: Since you are making choices all the time anyway, focus on making more active choices and fewer inactive choices.

Is your physical condition a system that needs attention? Then segregate it into manageable subsystems, and take first steps to improve those subsystems one at a time. Does a disorganized home system require attention? Acknowledge the disorder and begin to organize it, one room at a time.

Don't just sit there!

What Am I Not Doing Right Now?

How can you begin to use this action principle in your daily life, business, or job? Watch the events of your day as they occur, and while they are occurring, ask, "What am I *not* doing right now that is holding me back?" Should I stop and buy a small gift for the person I love? Should I find a way to exercise for an hour? Should I have a chat with a certain employee who seems a bit disconsolate lately? Shall I start, right this minute, to read that book I bought two months ago? Today, will I make an active effort to get control of things by writing a first draft of my Strategic Objective?

 The Power Is Out

Here is an example of placing a new subsystem between two dependent subsystems in order to gain a more reliable primary system. The story also illustrates how one can use a problem as a wake-up call to take action to make improvements.

Late in the afternoon on July 3, 2006, the electricity in Bend, Oregon, failed. A lightning strike had disabled a main transformer at the electric company substation on the edge of town. Linda and I were 160 miles to the north, in Portland, at a family Fourth of July celebration when Andi called to say that half of Bend was without electricity, including Centratel.

A rare event, the power outage did not present an immediate problem because Centratel's internal battery backup system automatically took over, keeping all telephone answering service computer systems operational.

The backup system has a three-hour capacity, so while the electricity was out, we held our breaths, hoping the power company crews would fix the problem quickly. They did, replacing the main transformer in just over two hours.

Over the years, it had been my experience that the occasional and infrequent power outages had been brief, and in this case, although the outage lasted longer than usual, our backup system yet again covered things perfectly. Without a hitch, our TSRs continued to process emergency calls during the outage.

But because of an aspect of our documented systems methodology, this was not the end of the story. Principle #7 of our 30 Principles document says: "Problems are gifts that inspire us to action. A problem prompts the act of creating or improving a system or procedure. We don't want setbacks, but when one occurs, we think, 'thank you for this wake-up call,' and take system-improvement action to prevent the setback from happening again."

Yes, our internal backup system worked flawlessly, but per that principle, we didn't breathe a sigh of relief and move on. Instead, we asked this question: "If we have only three hours of battery backup, what would happen in a worst-case scenario? What if the electricity was out for more than that, maybe an entire day, or longer?" That condition had not occurred in more than forty years because we reside in a region of the country where devastating storms are rare. But nonetheless, what if this outside system—the electric company that resides completely outside of our own control—experiences a catastrophic long-term failure?

We concluded that the possibility of a long-term outage was real, and for the welfare of our clients and the viability of the company itself, we had to consider the worst-case scenario. So we took the incident as a warning shot and decided we could not rely 100 percent on the electric company anymore. We had to be able to process calls without interruption, with or without externally supplied electricity.

The system solution? We purchased an on-site generator. The installation was a long, drawn-out, and expensive process, with numerous complications including structural challenges, permits from the city government, and finding the right people to do the work. But the new generator, which operates on either natural gas or propane, ensures that should a catastrophic power outage occur, we will be able to continue to process calls indefinitely. (Power outages don't typically cause telephone service to fail because telephone companies have their own backup generators.)

Per a recurring Microsoft Outlook task, one of our managers tests the generator once a month. Our staff have documented every single step of the generator activation process with "off the street" simplicity, and we always use that documentation in our testing exercises. (It's interesting that with each monthly test, invariably there are incremental improvements made in the lengthy written procedure. The Power Outage Working Procedure is a living thing, conforming to a changing environment and the tester's additional ideas for improvement.)

And how does this installation conform to the *Work the System* dictate of posturing oneself "outside and slightly elevated"? Perfectly. We inserted a generator between the power company and Centratel, creating the option of having independence from the outside power grid. Now we are outside and slightly elevated from the power company and no longer must we rely on a critical system that is not in our control.

Are you at the mercy of an outside system that repeatedly costs you time and money? Can you fix it or replace it? Can you eliminate it altogether?

CHAPTER 14

Quiet Courage

Faith is knowledge within the heart, beyond the reach of proof.

—KAHLIL GIBRAN

ALTHOUGH THERE ARE MANY POSSIBLE technical excuses for failure, it is a lack of what I call "quiet courage" that often precedes a downfall.

What is quiet courage? Quiet courage is unadorned action and it is the opposite of procrastination. A lack of quiet courage incites an error of omission. Quiet courage resides deep inside and causes one to buck up to do what needs to be done whether one wants to or not. Founded on internal fortitude, it is made real by self-discipline.

Understanding the quiet courage concept is, as usual, just a matter of digging a little deeper. Here are some demonstrations of quiet courage.

- Facing a misbehaving child in the evening with the same fairness and respect that was given to the child in the morning when the parent was fresh and far less tired.

- Going to work on a day when one just doesn't want to go to work.

- Facing up to a dead-end situation and taking action to address it once and for all.

- Exercising on a regular basis.

- Taking on a long-term, frustrating project, finding it even more draining than what was expected, but carrying on to finish anyway.

- Walking away from an argument with someone who is unreasonable.

- Living up to an agreement when it is more convenient to make excuses not to.

- Taking extra time to train an employee when things are busy.

- Making an organizational change when sitting still would be more acceptable to everyone else around you.

- Taking the time to create a Strategic Objective and a set of General Operating Principles, not to mention starting to put together a collection of Working Procedures.

The quiet-courage scenarios that escape notice are in contrast to the occasional overt courageous acts that earn instant recognition, such as challenging the boss with a delicate subject, approaching a neighbor with a legitimate but inflammatory complaint, or removing the delinquent young adult from the house.

Don't get me wrong: I'm a big fan of overt courageous acts; the more, the better. But never underestimate the damage caused by chronic, under-the-radar avoidance and procrastination.

Steady doses of quiet, unassuming courage, combined with the step-by-step system-improvement methodology, will take you where you want to go.

YOU CAN'T MEASURE NEGATIVE EVENTS THAT NEVER HAPPEN

Problems that will never happen can't sap your time and energy; they can't hold you back. Therefore, problems that will never occur have tangible value. But how can we measure future problems that won't happen—problems we can prevent before they can become reality? The answer is, it can't be done.

Measurement and stark objectivity are important, but an inability to measure should not stymie efforts to invest resources. This is where one must summon courage and common sense.

Here is an example of action based on—and in spite of—something that was immeasurable. At Centratel, the staff wage scale is close to 100 percent higher than our competitors'. How do we measure whether this elevated pay scale is a smart thing to do? The answer is we don't measure it because we can't measure it. Too many variables and too much subjectivity preclude analysis. Instead, we pay high wages because we have enough courage and common sense to know it is worth the extra cost.

At the beginning, it was tough to take this expensive subjective stance when a hard objective statistic—the total payroll dollars we paid out every two weeks—screamed for lower wages. An escalating payroll is easy to measure, but the benefits of the additional expenditure are impossible to pin down in hard numbers.

For instance, our high wages engender low staff turnover, which means less hiring and training. In dollars and cents, how does one measure the savings of the training costs that won't happen? Additionally, because of our superior quality staff, some quantity of error won't ever happen. How do we measure that?

And how does one gauge the value of customers *not* lost due to the poor quality that didn't occur? How many customers remain with us today who otherwise would have gone elsewhere?

So we invest time and money to prevent immeasurable negative events that won't happen, and to foster equally immeasurable positive events that will happen. This is quiet courage.

Yes, when it is possible and appropriate, we should measure, but just because a future condition is immeasurable doesn't mean action should not be taken.

PROCRASTINATION IS THE EVIL ONE

At Centratel and at home, the quiet courage posture is easy for me because it aligns with the rest of the *Work the System* philosophy. It's a learned habit, ingrained by simple Pavlovian positive reinforcement: It works, so I do it.

When Centratel was just moments away from collapse, finding the wherewithal to summon up quiet and not-so-quiet courage was not a problem because there was a gun to my head. The loss of everything was a vision just in front of my face, and I exhibited the same visceral protective reaction I would display if someone were pushing me toward the edge of a cliff. As Henry Ford put it, "The greatest inspiration is often born of desperation."

But without the presence of a gun-to-the-head motivator, and when making excuses is enticing, I can see that quiet courage's number one nemesis, procrastination, is at work once again. The antidote is the point-of-sale action posture (we'll talk about that in the next chapter).

Here are two cognitive strategies for when the internal battle rages.

The first strategy is to rise above it and visualize laziness as an object, something tangible that is outside of you. Once the mechanical laziness is observed—most often it is temporary indolence cloaked by some lame excuse such as "I'm too busy right now" or "I'm too tired"—just ignore the external seduction and get moving without a second thought.

The second strategy to use as the excuses line themselves up is to ask, "Why am I lacking courage at this moment? Why am I being a *sissy?*" It's a bit of twisted psychology that rattles the cage and causes a passionate reaction. Of all human failures, perhaps cowardice is the most abhorred. Procrastination—that is, the lack of quiet courage—will ruin your life if you let it.

 ## You Will Begin Now

Here is a real-time, outside-and-slightly-elevated exercise. It's about what is happening right NOW. Here, *you* are the story.

Anyone can read a book, but it's a courageous act to shift in a new direction. Clearly, because you have read this far, implementing the *Work the System* methodology is a new life trajectory you are considering.

How do you get to the point of actually beginning the process without relegating it to a future date when spare time is available? Here's how: Right now—this second—put this book down—yes, right now, *this* second. Find a blank piece of paper and write "Strategic Objective" at the top. Do it.

Now, place the paper in a location where you will easily find it later.

Congratulations! Your pilgrimage has begun! My bet is you will get back to your titled paper sooner rather than later. Why? Because you have begun, and beginning is the hardest part.

CHAPTER 15

Point-of-Sale Thinking

Why? Because I'm the mommy, and I said so.

—ANONYMOUS MOMMY

DO IT NOW AND LET'S GET ON WITH WHATEVER IS NEXT!

Point-of-sale is a phrase taken from the cash register industry. It describes action "where the purchase takes place."

Consider the latest generation of cash register, which instantly updates inventory and orders new product. Before the customer walks away from the till, a replacement for the purchased item has been ordered and all internal accounting is completed. The concept is a key component of the *Work the System* method as described in our Operating Principles document, Principle #14: "Do it NOW. All actions build on 'point-of-sale' theory. We don't delay an action if it can be done immediately. Just like any major retail outlet, we 'update databases and inventories at the exact time the transaction takes place.' There is no paperwork floating around the office after a physical transaction. We ask, 'How can we perform the task NOW without creating lingering details that we must clean up later?'"

The concept of point-of-sale, with its various subtleties, has the single purpose of gobbling up details and tasks as they arise. Accomplishing this is the antithesis of fire-killing. Point-of-sale means being in the offense, eyes open, ready to handle whatever comes up, instead of defensively looking backward, burning up precious time sorting through piles of old details.

For both your business and your personal life, the point-of-sale posture allows you to focus on the path ahead while your other systems strategies take care of the details that come behind. Wear the point-of-sale banner on your sleeve and you will experience robust confidence, the opposite of overwhelm. The excuses "I don't have enough time" and "I've been too busy" will disappear from your life.

In a nutshell, here are two point-of-sale strategies that will make your life simple and clean. The first is to reject procrastination. Get tasks out of the way *now* by immediately doing them, delegating them, or discarding them. Make it your quest to *knock off tasks as they appear!* The second strategy is to eliminate the requirement for personal action by automating and systemizing tasks. By making things happen automatically, the "do it now" goal is achieved without any effort at all.

Here's an additional benefit of the point-of-sale stance: You will be in an alert, assertive posture, prepared to handle the inevitable bodyslams that are part of having a life.

Your Conga Line Dance Leadership

Embracing the point-of-sale stance makes you the first person in the metaphorical conga line, the one determining the line's trajectory and speed. The dozens of followers just shadow your movements. The conga line goes where you want it to go despite the disparity in shape, size, and finesse of the dancers who follow. You are at the front, the leader, forging the path ahead while the gyrations that emerge behind sort themselves out on their own. The "system principles" for the members of the conga line are simply to keep their hands on the hips of the preceding dancer and to keep in step—and to follow your lead.

IT'S JUST THE WAY WE DO THINGS AROUND HERE

When the "Shall I do it now or later?" question comes up for a new Centratel staff member, their not-yet-disciplined internal dialogue goes something like this: "What's the difference if I do this task now or later? I just don't *feel* like doing it right now. I'll do it later because my guess is I will feel more like doing it then." A variation is: "I function better under pressure. I need an imminent deadline to force me to take action, so I'll do this task next week when that deadline arrives (or, maybe, the task will miraculously disappear by then)." Sound familiar?

During job orientation, we ask the new staff member to change that internal self-talk to "I'll do it *now* because that is how things are done at Centratel."

Our experienced managers embrace the "do it now" credo because it is so potently effective, not just because it's our policy, but because it just works! No need for self-explanation; no time for inane back-and-forth internal dialogue. The posture is, "Do it NOW and let's get on with things!"

Yes, this "because I said so" dictate may grate a bit, especially in the milieu of independence and freedom we Westerners take for granted. We don't like arbitrary rules imposed by others, but in a business setting, an employee has the freedom to quit if the rules don't seem reasonable. In the free world, anyone can leave a job to go to work for someone else, start a new business, or sit on the couch and do nothing.

But for the new Centratel employee, once he or she tests a concept and its workability is proven, it's a no-brainer; it's logic. Consistently superior end results are justification for cast-in-concrete methodology.

Of course, the point-of-sale concept also spills over into personal life decisions. Here's an oversimplification, but it captures the point: "I'm shopping. While I'm out, should I make one more stop to buy groceries for tomorrow?" The answer, of course, is "Yes!"

Multitasking Is for Machines

The goal of the point-of-sale strategy is to create superefficient primary systems. However, it is important to remember that in a point-of-sale cash register, the all-at-the-same-time tasks are *automated*. Multitasking, or "many systems functioning at one time," is a perfect application for a computer, not a human being. Let your Mac or PC do the multitasking. In fact, a tenet of Centratel's philosophy is that our staff members do *not* multitask; rather, they "give full attention . . . to the detail at hand" (Principle #27). This means proceeding in a linear format.

THE WORKWEEK IS FORTY HOURS LONG

The *Work the System* methodology produces many system strategies that save time, and there is no question that point-of-sale thinking has much to do with keeping our salaried management staff's workweek to a reasonable length. My partner and I say to our employees, "Here's the deal: If you give us 100 percent, we will compensate you well." Yes, it's a generalized promise, but nonetheless it is our personal guarantee to staff that when they work hard *and* produce, we will provide them a healthy wage, great benefits, and a workweek of reasonable length.

Because of our procedure-driven, point-of-sale methodology, our people do not see the fifty- to sixty-hour (or more) workweeks that are common in small- to medium-size service businesses like ours. Why do my partner and I require that well-paid, salaried employees work no more than forty hours a week? First, we want them to have a life outside the business. And second, when they have time to unwind, they are fresh and spunky when they return to work, able to give the required 100 percent that is part of "the deal."

COMMUNICATIONS AND POINT OF SALE

Point-of-sale methodology is at the heart of our personal communications strategy, too. Fine ideas can flow quickly through the thought process without being captured. One might be driving, talking to a colleague, lying in bed, riding a bicycle, or traveling cross-country when a great idea arrives out of nowhere only to depart in the next instant. That's why I carry a digital voice recorder with me everywhere. Fleeting though they may be, creative ideas are too valuable to lose.

Be Cold-blooded: What Really Matters?

In your business or job, or in your personal life, how much of what you do *really* matters? This is not a loaded question; it is one of enormous pragmatic consideration. Be cold-blooded in examining your situation and eliminating the thoughts, data, and preoccupations that don't have value.

Also, look hard at the information that is of *some* value. See if it serves *enough* value to make its existence worthwhile. If any information you receive is not used, or is of marginal use, categorize it for what it is—a waste of time, energy, and/or money—and then dismiss it from your life.

What will you do with the time you save? You'll expend it on things that *do* matter.

STRENGTHENING THE HABIT

Procrastination (here it is again!) appears in the low times, the times when personal willpower is weak because of stress, fatigue, problems, and distractions. Failing to carry through with the point-of-sale philosophy is often the first casualty. You think, "Okay, I understand that in the long run, point-of-sale is a good concept, but this afternoon I'm tired, and there is always tomorrow . . ."

You are probably right. More often than not, a task *can* happen tomorrow. The danger is that when one compromises a habit, the habit becomes weaker. But when an excuse not to do something arrives, yet you do it anyway, the do-it-now habit becomes incrementally stronger.

In everything you do, think beyond immediate temptation and stick with the plan as outlined in your critical documents. Your documentation will keep you from sinking as it relentlessly moves you toward your goals!

Point-of-sale actions are about self-discipline and the willingness to stretch into uncomfortable territory. How else can things change for the better?

SLOW DOWN; GET ORGANIZED

Too many people live in the chaos brought about by the failure to slow down enough to set goals and determine sensible strategies to reach those goals. Add to this the failure to make system improvements when inefficiencies crop up, which would prevent those problems from recurring.

Yes, the key phrase is "slow down" and—let me guess—slowing down is what you are struggling with right now as you work your way through this book. If at first slowing down doesn't feel right, that's normal. Be patient as you work your systems and the end result will be fast, efficient processes down the line.

I learned this potent mind-set on my high school ski team while training for slalom, a discipline that requires forethought, fast reflexes, strength, and balance. I used to slam through the gates with abandon, powering my way down the course off balance, my arms and legs flailing. I was giving it everything, but my race results were mediocre because of the multiple errors and inefficiencies generated by my brute-force, hell-bent approach. I was making too many tiny mistakes that incrementally slowed me down, or I was outright crashing and not even finishing.

Then one day my coach told me to relax, to think "smooth and slow" instead of "power," as I skied down through the slalom gates. At first it felt wrong, and it was frustrating because it seemed to me I was not *trying* hard enough. But I forced myself to hold back, to ski slowly and smoothly. My results dramatically improved. From then on, including two years on a college team, I seldom failed to finish a race and consistently ranked well. The "slow down and be smooth" lesson spilled over into the rest of my life, too. (But even after all these years, I occasionally struggle with this positioning because my natural inclination is to thrash things into orderliness.)

 Measure Your Body

I mentioned this earlier but I want to go into more detail: Nine years ago, in the depths of my workplace chaos, I was also dealing with a very sick body and an exhausted mind. I was delirious during the day and couldn't sleep at night. My doctor had me on antidepressants, then Ritalin, convinced I was "depressed"—my hundred-hour workweeks notwithstanding!

But as a result of my mini-enlightenment regarding the systems of my business, I grasped that my body was likewise a collection of systems. I asked, "What are my body's systems composed of?" It was obvious: The human body is composed of chemicals. Armed with this realization, I asked my doctor to give me a wide range of blood tests. Convinced of my "depression," at first he balked at the idea, but then he conceded.

The blood analysis showed that my adrenal glands had shut down and my master hormone, DHEA, was not in evidence. The "stress hormone," Cortisol, was in the stratosphere, another important hormone was deficient, and I was chronically dehydrated.

My task was to work on each of the systems individually and, one by one, bring each back to normalcy. Once I got all four dysfunctional systems back to efficiency, I would have a balanced, holistic body and an alert mind. How could it be otherwise?

For the next two years, I took blood tests repeatedly while I faithfully took supplements and modified my lifestyle, bringing my various chemical systems back into balance. At the end of that time period, I was physically strong and my thinking was clear.

Was it that simple? Yes and no. On the one hand, the road to recovery was obvious—*what* I had to do was clear. On the other hand, it was sometimes a struggle to be self-disciplined enough to do what needed to be done. I stumbled once in awhile, but I succeeded enough to improve things dramatically. Do I still stumble? Yes!

How about you? Are you sure the chemicals that compose your body are okay? If they are not, could this be affecting your physical and mental performance? Consider taking your health into your own hands by directing your doctor to perform full-screen blood tests. Then again, your solution may not require a doctor. If your chemicals are okay, maybe you just need to get regular exercise, eat better, and find more sleep.

A final thought about measuring your body. If you are addicted to a substance, however benign, an imbalance exists. Any foreign substance throws things off, so a good starting point is to quit those substances and face the world "cold turkey." It may not be easy, but if you can pull it off, you'll be in select company.

There is no better place than one's body to start getting things straightened out. Using systems strategy to analyze the physical body—the vehicle that holds and transports consciousness—is perhaps the most outside-and-slightly-elevated position one can take.

Hard questions: *Are you moving too fast? If so, what steps can you take so your life slows down? What's your addiction? Do you think it is hampering your forward motion?*

CHAPTER 16

Extraordinary Systems
Operated by Great People

Most people, especially successful people, are hard working.
They want to participate. They want to do things well.

—ANNIE LEIBOVITZ

I'VE DISCUSSED THE IMPORTANCE of creating efficient, documented systems but have not sufficiently addressed a prime benefit: Your superb systems are for regular people like you and me, people who do not have super powers.

People have said to me, "I'm sure you are successful because you've been lucky enough to find very good people to work for you." Translation: "You just stumbled into finding people who adore you, know your every thought, and will perform your every wish. You lucky guy!"

The idea that one must "find the right people" is a pervasive misconception. It is not that the statement isn't true; it's that the inference is backward. At Centratel, we *do* have an extraordinary staff from top to bottom, but that is not because of plain dumb luck or my prowess as a recruiter. It's because we attract and keep quality people due to the great work situation we offer. The great situation comes *before* the great people.

Plenty of hardworking, disciplined, honest people are out there, quietly looking for a fair shake so they can put themselves on the line and show what they can do. And when they perform well, they want to be rewarded. You just need to attract these people and then give them black-and-white instruction, good pay, and the promise of a bright future. As always, it's just simple mechanics.

Seeking the perfect employee who will solve all problems—a from-the-top-down solution—is the opposite of the systems-thinking solution. In the *Work the System* business, your job as a leader is to provide an exceptional business system that will attract hardworking, loyal, and long-term employees—a from-the-bottom-up solution.

So these great people *become* great employees. You make it possible for them to shine by providing a forum for their innate skills and high motivation. You give them opportunity and turn them loose.

Assertively Apply the Guidelines

Avoid the danger of becoming bogged down in the pros and cons of a decision. Accomplish this by assertively applying the guidelines of the three critical documents.

At Centratel, I love it when a new employee explains that he or she is taking a certain action because it is congruent with a guideline within the Strategic Objective, the 30 Principles document, or a particular Working Procedure.

Another positive sign is a staff member's unsolicited request for a Working Procedure's modification—a sure indication he or she "gets" the systems methodology.

TO THESE PEOPLE YOU OWE YOUR BEST

You want smart, honest, clean-living, and enthusiastic people who will believe in what you have created; individuals who can become intrigued with your personal vision and who will want to continue into the future with you—at least for a while. These good people are the bedrock of your future. To them you owe the best—and the best's centerpiece is the carefully constructed system-based environment you provide. Then, if your people grow with your company and you teach them well, it will be a compliment to you if someday they go out and start their own businesses. On the other hand, it will be the supreme compliment if they stay with you over the long term.

Is the Focus on the Product or the System?

It seems logical that any manager's total efforts should be focused on the product or service itself. That is, all of that person's energy should be directed to the work that must be done, the customers who must be found, and the money that must be made. But this is the problem! Focus entirely on these tasks without an overall strategy of system improvement, and dysfunction is imminent. Failure to adopt an outside-and-slightly-elevated perspective is the primary reason only one business out of one hundred will survive fifteen years. Here's good news: The bulk of those 1 percent survivors are doing very well indeed. Albeit morbid, here's more good news for you: The vast majority of your new competitors are doomed.

Understand what large successful businesses have in common: The leader is *not* producing the product or service. He or she is holding court, observing and adjusting the systems that produce and market the product or service. To accomplish this, the leader insists that the company's managers document goals, principles, and procedures—and ensures that employees follow this documentation exactly.

EVALUATING PEOPLE

Your team must see things your way. If you are going to embrace the *Work the System* method and you are in charge of staff, you will have to remove people who can't or won't deal with your vision. Then you will replace them with new people who share your systems mind-set.

In our search for system-oriented personalities at Centratel, here are a few "hoops" that job applicants must negotiate. Note that clearheadedness and self-discipline are the common threads of these systems-thinking prerequisites:

1. Did the applicant show up for the interview on time?
2. Was the minimum score achieved on the aptitude test?
3. Does the applicant know about the business? Did he or she check out the website before applying for the position? Are there

questions about what goes on, or is the applicant just looking for *any* job? Is advancement important?

4. Did the interviewee smile? Seem happy? Generally, did he or she seem to be self-disciplined?

5. Did the applicant *listen* to you or were your words sliding by unheard as the person waited for the next opportunity to pitch his or her expertise?

6. Can the interviewee carry on a reasonable conversation? Did he or she look you in the eye when speaking?

7. Did the applicant's appearance convey that she or he takes care of herself or himself? If not, the raw truth is that in most cases of personal neglect, there is a corresponding lack of self-discipline.

8. Did the applicant previously bounce from job to job?

9. Did the interviewee pass the drug test?

10. Does the applicant naturally play by the rules? Did he or she pass the criminal background check?

By breaking down the subjective interview process into component parts, we transform it into an objective, black-and-white test. Yes, intuition can be important, but it should never overrule your guidelines. Don't confuse feelings with logic, subjectivity with objectivity. However compassionate, the "this person needs a break" gut feeling is too often a mistake. Use such a feeling to disqualify rather than to qualify people. (That's a useful rule to follow elsewhere in life, too.)

At Centratel, it is critical that the job applicant pass through *all* of the aforementioned "hoops." If he or she fails just one, we won't offer the position because that one negative indicator probably points to a problem that can't be neutralized even by all the other positive signals added together. We are hard-hearted about this and don't make exceptions.

College education? We don't worry too much about this, although a college degree indicates someone who can stick through long-term challenges to reach a goal. Unfortunately, a college degree is no longer a reliable barometer of literate capability or of a reasonable mind-set.

You know this already: Hiring and then firing someone is not just a bad investment for the company, it's also an intense personal blow to the employee. For the job prospect, it's infinitely less painful to not get the job in the first place. Be compassionate by creating a thoughtful (and, of course, documented) hiring procedure.

KILL THE MOLES, MANAGE THE FLEET

And what about the leader of a typical large, successful company? Most times, these people are not innately special. Beyond their willingness to work hard and an adequate degree of intelligence, their leg up is that they naturally operate from a systems perspective—while the huge majority of people do not. These leaders are heavyweights because they understand that moles must be eliminated, not repeatedly whacked.

The systems perspective is already permanently etched into the minds of those who manage large, successful organizations, but the interesting thing is that it is such a simple concept, many of the people who innately embrace it can't describe it, much less identify it as the critical factor of their success.

Via managers who understand the process, the large-business leader focuses on perfecting systems and keeping them that way, constantly making efficiency adjustments while simultaneously keeping up with trends and changes. It should be the same for you if you are to climb out of the morass within which 95 percent of the world struggles.

For your business, you must find and keep employees and suppliers, supervise the creation and sales of your product or service, make payroll, pay taxes, and steer the whole enterprise toward a profit. If you are to leap ahead, your product or service must be consistently superior, and that can't happen if your people don't hyperfocus on the details of how that product or service is produced and distributed.

In the short term, you must focus on creating extraordinary, well-defined systems. In the long term, you and your staff must relentlessly tweak and maintain those systems. The by-product will be an extraordinary service or product that people want.

Another thought: *All* the ships in your fleet must be at peak efficiency. One slow boat will hold back the entire flotilla. This is a central tenet of the *Work the System* method, and it's the reason you will want to ensure that all your people are on board with your systems methodology. You'll want everyone in your organization working at peak capacity, repairing, tweaking, and adjusting to outside changes. The fleet must move forward full steam, directly toward the common goal, and it is your job to make sure that happens. This is called "being a leader."

If you hold a job and your goal is to advance, you have equal challenges. To win in the long term you must do things more efficiently than your competition or your peers, and you can't be more efficient by winging it, depending on personal charm, trying to be the perfect employee, or doing things like everyone else.

 ## A Super Market

Being aware of the systems around you, and of distinguishing the efficient from the inefficient, keeps your systems mind-set front and center.

In southern California there is a certain grocery store chain that passionately ensures that all of its markets are organized and relaxed. The rows of goods are full. Everything is clean and polished. In fact, the people who work there are clean and polished! Walk the aisles and catch the eye of a clerk. You can feel the pride.

Each store is efficient, confident in itself. I don't know the top management people, but it's obvious: Here is a perfect model of thought-out and documented systems strategy, directed from the top of the organization down to the customer-contact level.

Of course, other businesses just like this one exist. They are not common, but you will find them. When you do, spend time there and think about the systems that are behind the efficiencies. Watch and learn.

It's easy to find floundering businesses. You can't help spending time in them because they are everywhere. In visiting such businesses, there is also much to learn. Get a visceral feeling for the lack of systems and vision, the lack of controls. Feel the chaos. This is the antithesis of what you want for your work and your life.

In your personal experience, can you think of a superefficient business? Can you identify systems that have been set up that cause and maintain this efficiency? Are the people working within this business alert, busy, and happy?

CHAPTER 17

Consistency and Cold Coffee

My goal in sailing isn't to be brilliant or flashy in individual
races, just to be consistent over the long run.

—Dennis Conner

In the Pacific Northwest, the coffee kiosk is pervasive. Often smaller than a hundred square feet in size, these tiny portable buildings inhabit parking lots adjacent to busy intersections and high-traffic streets. Typically operated by perky, bright-eyed "baristas," the kiosks are convenient for the drive-up-on-a-whim coffee drinker. The concoctions they serve run the gauntlet of complexity and can cost as much as $8. Although the kiosks offer every coffee drink imaginable, I don't often use them. The infrequent times I drink coffee, I go out of my way to buy it at either a national franchise (guess who?) downtown or a locally operated shop that serves equally good coffee, with a preference for the local shop (because, well, it's local).

About ten years ago, in the midst of my hundred-hour workweeks, I experimented with patronizing a new kiosk near my home. On the way to work one morning, I pulled over, desperate for a cup of strong, hot coffee.

The barista reached down to my car window and served me my coffee in a paper cup. I set the cup in the holder, negotiated my car back onto the busy street, and was again on my way to the office. I was *so* ready for that first sip and . . . Yeck! It was tepid, thin, and tasteless. Arrggghhh! I instantly ratcheted to ten on the frustration level—and have always remembered the intensity of my annoyance with that particular cup of coffee.

I drove downtown to one of my standby shops, and with a ceremonial flourish, dumped the still-full kiosk cup in the trash bin outside. I stepped inside and bought another cup.

As usual at this shop, the coffee was hot and strong. I remember my satisfaction with *that* particular cup.

Here's the aftermath that, to this day, still surprises me: I shy away from buying coffee at a kiosk. Why? Am I being too critical, too unforgiving? Neither—it's more self-serving than that. It's because I don't want to deal with the inconvenience again, and especially, I don't want to feel like a fool for making the same mistake twice.

So, after all these years, my first impulse is to avoid patronizing a kiosk if one of my regular coffee shops is within five miles. And my visceral aversion falls on a number of other local establishments too, including half a dozen restaurants, as many retail stores, and more than one gas station. To be sure, my gut-level judgments are not completely fair or entirely rational, but they are real.

Centratel is a pure service operation, so quality of service is my natural mind-set. When out and about, I find myself evaluating the service quality of restaurants, sandwich shops, retail stores, movie theaters, plumbers, bed and breakfasts, public transportation services, etc. It's an unconscious analysis until I encounter superb service or poor service, at which point I automatically get conscious. On the spot, I have offered jobs to friendly, smart, and upbeat servers or cashiers who can't keep smiles off their faces. Then there are the other times when someone with a lousy attitude forever alienates me from that establishment.

Outside of work, my managers naturally do this evaluation, too. Once the systems mind-set takes hold, it's impossible to avoid.

In fairness to kiosk operators: Just before the publication of this book, one of my managers informed me that Centratel's "Latte Monday" drinks (we buy coffee or cocoa drinks for everyone on busy Monday mornings) are now being provided by a kiosk, not one of the local shops, as had been our tradition. Our staff members say the kiosk drinks are consistently superb. Could it be this particular kiosk has something special going on? Could it be it is being operated differently than the "cold cup" kiosk of so many years ago?

The answer to both questions is obviously yes. Why was the coffee so poor at the "cold cup" kiosk? The proprietor had no procedures installed to ensure consistent quality. She had no clue she had to consciously manipulate systems in order to keep customers. Further, she had no idea of the enormous negative impact of one bad cup of coffee. I am sure she winged it every day, hoping for the best but more often hitting-and-missing, depending on her emotions, the attitude of her customers, or even the weather. The result? The kiosk went out of business after just a short time.

WATCHING YOURSELF CLOSELY

In observing my own overreaction to that single cup of cold coffee, I learned something: It was clear to me the success of Centratel was going to depend on our ability to provide *consistent* high quality.

What if you work for someone else? That's easy, and here's the mantra: "My boss is my primary customer. At work, my number one task is to avoid letting my boss down." (Of course, if the boss is impossible, or the position is dead-end, exiting the situation is probably a better strategy.)

The bad news is true. In our culture, and despite the universe's propensity for efficiency, service quality is too often poor, mostly because of the human tendency to neglect systems. But the good news is that it's easy to provide superb service if the focus is on creating and maintaining systems that will ensure consistent quality.

Here it is yet again: Creation, maintenance, and improvement of internal systems must be the manager's main objective.

The following is a not so tongue-in-cheek "for instance": You don't want a customer treated badly by an employee who has a hangover. What you want is a system that will cover the bases for someone who is having a bad day (presuming this someone is not a chronic problem employee). You can't stop the person's headache, but you can create solid, fluid, and sensible procedures that will get this employee through the shift without alienating customers. Not providing guidance and leaving things up to your not-doing-so-well-today employee is a losing bet—the numbers do not bode well for you, the business owner or department manager.

And what if *you* have a hangover? If you have worked your systems, you can sit back for a day or so, stay out of the way without gumming up the works with your sour disposition, and let your systems carry the load.

It's a powerful human idiosyncrasy, this willingness to make snap yet irreversible negative decisions based on one-time bad experiences. So beware: When customers are disappointed in service, they will have a predilection to go elsewhere next time, never to return. Your best bet is to not fail them in the first place.

The Tip System

Here is an evaluation system, albeit waggish. It's about tipping in restaurants, and I'll preface things by saying I don't believe a tip is a diner's obligation. It's a *tip*—something extra that one earns if the service he or she delivers is at least good.

Linda and I sit down for a meal in a restaurant. At this point, before even saying a word, the waitperson, in this case a female, has earned a 25 percent tip. It's downhill from there. If she greets us with "how are you *guys* today?" there is an immediate 5 percent deduction in the tip for offhandedly calling Linda a "guy." Now the tip can be no more than 20 percent. If the waitperson delivers the food and walks away with a semi-pretentious, airheaded "enjoy," there is another 5 percent discount. If she delivers the check along with the food (workingman's diners excepted), there's another 5 percent off the top. If she checks to see how we are doing at mid-meal and blatantly interrupts one of us midsentence, yes, there is another 5 percent deduction. Now we're approaching no tip at all.

Although I don't sit there tallying things on paper, or even in my head, and seldom does a waitperson go without being tipped, the essence of my thinking process is in the above formula. Call me persnickety. It is systems thinking both at its best and at its most ridiculous.

How does this relate? If I were the owner of a restaurant, understanding that serving food is a process that repeats itself, I would be watching my own reactions while dining at someone else's restaurant. I'd take notes. In my own restaurant, I would produce a Working Procedure of "never use" phrases and actions and then would make sure every single one of my servers knew it by heart. It would be called the Forbidden Phrases and Actions Procedure. (Yes, really. That is exactly what I would call it.) This Working Procedure would be my obsession and my staff's center of attention. We would continuously update it, using my own experience as well as feedback from customers, open-eyed staff, or whomever. Only one or two pages in length, it would be *alive*; the continuous centerpiece of discussion and action, a document that old hands and new people would study, discuss, and tweak. With everyone's input it would improve steadily over time. I would post it prominently in the kitchen, in the back offices, and the lounge. We would relentlessly "work the system" to higher and higher efficiency and usefulness.

For the owner of a restaurant, how much work is this? A simple document like this could quickly take a restaurant's service quality from mediocre to superb—an incredible payback for a tiny investment of time and effort.

Can you think of work situations like this, situations that repeat themselves over and over yet always seem to have a different response depending on who is handling the situation?

WE WATCH AND LEARN

At Centratel, we watch and learn and we use that information in our work and in our personal lives. We try hard to avoid foul-ups, but when we do commit an error, we are finicky about fixing it. We bombard the unhappy customer with tender loving care to the point where he or she is happier after the error than before it. (Via our Complaint Procedure, we call the customer back a minimum of four times, at prescribed intervals of one day, three days, ten days, and thirty days, to make sure the error has not repeated itself. Yes, that process of fixing things is via a 1-2-3-step documented system.)

Our Complaint Procedure doesn't end there. We also inform the *entire* staff of *every* complaint, as well as the steps taken to remedy less-than-perfect situations.

So you don't operate a business? If you are someone's employee and your position has potential, apply these principles and watch your rapid ascent of the corporate ladder.

TWEAKING AND MAINTAINING

So the primary commonality among large, successful businesses is the steady, concerted effort to maintain consistency in product and service quality. This means that in a prosperous business the leader spends *most* of his or her time supervising the tweaking and maintaining of subsystems. The more successful a business is in gaining and retaining customers, the more one can be sure that that business has a strict set of system guidelines for quality control and customer service. Again, for the successful employee aiming to climb the corporate ladder, this system-improvement process is also the center of attention (although confined to one's area of responsibility rather than to an entire company).

Just how hard can I beat this concept to death? It's all about perfecting systems and then maintaining that perfection!

What about your personal life? It's what Mom told you: Always return a friend's phone call promptly. Say thank you, pay your bills on time, and pay attention to holidays. Don't forget birthdays. If you promise something, make sure you do it no matter how trivial. Do these things consistently and people will trust you. They will want to help you. They will know you are dependable and will want to spend time with you.

A Place for Everything and Everything in Its Place

Work the System methodology relies on the personal habit of consistency, the child of character and self-discipline. Consistency is not a hand tool one picks up from the tool bench to use only when needed; it is a personal trait to pack around everywhere, a trait to be used every minute, permanently embedded in the fiber of your being.

To cultivate this trait, the largest challenge is to fight old habits, simple laziness and procrastination, while channeling moment-to-moment activities into organized, efficient systems. However, by paying attention, good results come home quickly. With those successes, you'll find that consistency soon becomes effortless, and backtracking into old habits dissatisfying.

It is no good to set up a system of organization at work and then return home to chaos. It doesn't work to exercise a few days of the month, be nice to your spouse most of the time, or to apply the *Work the System* principles sporadically. If life is to be efficient, maintaining your systems and staying organized is a full-time job.

Fifty years ago, my grandfather carefully explained, "Sam, there is a place for everything and everything in its place." I was eight years old then and I wondered how Grandpa knew his favorite platitude was true, and why he seemed so caught up in the idea. Was there *proof* this was a good idea?

His simple explanation was *it's just true that being organized is worthwhile.* At first, if you must, take it on faith that being organized is something good. Then, find the time tomorrow to clean that top drawer in your desk, and this weekend, go out to the garage and start the cleanup. Do some organizing every day even if it's for just fifteen minutes each time. Work on the old clutter but also, from this point forward, avoid creating new clutter as you move through the day. It might take weeks or months to take care of getting things in order, but this is what you must do to drop into the groove of the systems mentality. Accomplish this cleanup and then step back and ask yourself how you feel. There will be intense satisfaction, and the great thing is, this satisfaction is addicting; you'll want to feel it again and again. Keep at it and soon disorder will bother you. You'll become a fanatic about organization and systems thinking as you discover that your world is becoming smooth and efficient. *Be consistent, and with consistency comes strength.*

Plow through the disorder in your life and you will find the process is exactly congruent with the other aspects of the *Work the System* method. You'll see disorganization in the people and places around you—disorganization you can't fix—and you will shake your head as you understand the waste of it.

Will your new orderliness make you an uptight control freak? No, on the contrary, as I pointed out in the beginning of the book, you'll loosen up and feel relaxed and effective. You'll be a smooth operator with time and energy to spare.

Breaking the Rules and Job Security

The following example has nothing to do with "good" or "bad" employees, or about discipline or conflict resolution. Simply, it has to do with thorough documentation and staff buy-in. With clear-cut rules, no gray areas exist to cause uncertainty or anxiety.

Several years ago we had problems with two Centratel employees. The first one's work was very good, but he failed a random drug test. The second one's work quality was also exceptional, but she violated our computer privacy policy. Both instances were serious breaches of the company's written guidelines.

What to do? It crossed our minds that we could sweep these major offenses under the carpet in order to spare unpleasantness and eliminate a time-consuming search for replacements. But we had to ask, if we keep employees who violate policy, wouldn't this render our policies impotent?

The system solution? We spell out rules, regulations, and guidelines in our Employee Handbook, viewing this collection of policies as a primary system in itself—a giant Working Procedure. (You can find the entire 35,000-word document at centratel.com, under Resources.) All employees are required to understand the company's policies and, by signing a statement, show that they accept them as a condition of employment.

Per the handbook, these serious violations were cause for employment termination. And that's what happened. We ended their employment on the spot. There was no arbitrary, manipulative corporate judgment call. We simply followed the "conditions of employment" system that had been set up in advance.

Our system allows management to be completely objective, remaining outside of any emotional or manipulative positioning. The Employee Handbook spells our policies out exactly and explains the ramifications of not following them. These two employees knew they were gambling. They lost their respective gambles and their departures were simple and clean. Parties on both sides—and our remaining staff—understood why these terminations occurred.

Because we follow policies exactly, all Centratel employees know that a deliberate act of crossing the line will not be met with wishy-washy "don't let it happen again" platitudes or interminable second chances. After a serious violation, does an employee deserve a second chance? Well, actually, no, as a matter of policy they don't. But because of this intractable position, policy violations seldom arise and we are not often faced with letting someone go.

Employees want rules to be consistent and fair, and in contrast to some conventional corporate wisdom, my partner and I believe that when we let someone go for assertively violating clear-cut policy, our remaining employees feel *more* secure in their jobs, not less. Yes, we lost two valuable people, but the losses were outweighed by the positive, long-term effects on the remaining rule-abiding staff who always understand where things stand and that management is fair.

There is an important subtlety here that I want to clarify: Did we terminate the employment of these two individuals to set an example? No. We terminated their employment because "that's the deal." If an example was set, it was a by-product of the action.

Do you see recurring negative situations with the people in your workplace where clarification on paper would eliminate future contention? Does it make sense that establishing clear-cut rules in advance—before any contentious situation has occurred—would dramatically eliminate future conflict?

CHAPTER 18

Communication: Grease for the Wheels

*The quality of your communication equals
the quality of your life.*

—Anthony Robbins

It seems sensible that a discussion of communication would parallel other *Work the System* protocols, protocols that dictate that quality supersedes quantity. However, I disagree with this. The sense I have developed over the years is that *quantity* of communication is more important than *quality* of communication. (By the way, I am referring here to sensible discourse between two parties. It is no good if one party spews enormous amounts of useless information while ignoring the other side.)

Quantity of communication connects directly to any success or failure.

Is someone talking and someone else listening? Or is there silence? Simply looking at world affairs confirms that between nations, the degree of cooperation is in direct proportion to the *amount* of two-way communication that occurs. Paranoia ensues if exchange is limited.

It's the same in a marriage or a workplace relationship. More communication leads to better efficiency, stronger cooperation, and deeper trust. Between two people—or between two nations—if silence reigns, problems will arise in the relationship, or there will be no relationship at all. Of course, if one party is crazy, communicating can become worse than a waste of time; it can be damaging.

If lots of communication occurs, the quality will take care of itself. Because our regular communication at Centratel is so thorough I am sometimes at a loss for agenda topics for our weekly staff meetings. Nevertheless, we meet every Monday morning even if it's just to chat about an upcoming wedding or someone's camping trip. It keeps us in touch and we feel like a team. We laugh, and that alone is worth it. We keep the meeting short, though. We have work to do.

I have ad hoc get-togethers now and then—in person, by teleconference, or by phone—with my two senior managers, Andi and Hollee, who have the deepest understanding of the company's overall systems strategy. These meetings go to the root of things. Our discussions are fluid and concise, and in a very few minutes we discuss a variety of issues. My partner, Sam, and I have occasional quick check-in chats too, pointed and brief.

There is a caveat (there's always a caveat) to the idea that quantity trumps quality, however: communication with oneself—one's own personal self-talk. Here, excessive internal communication is a problem, especially in Western culture. We examine, re-examine, dissect, and massage our personal thoughts, endlessly wondering, What *is* the problem? Is he (or she) angry with me? Did I say something wrong? Did I do enough? Do I need medication? Am I a good person? Argh! We could do well to act more and self-ruminate less.

You can improve the external, mechanical aspects of communication with yourself. Shortly after we turned things around at Centratel, I devised a personal point-of-sale communication system that is enormously efficient. Using a cellular phone, Microsoft Outlook, and a voice recorder helps me cover a lot of ground, easily doubling my overall effectiveness. (See worthesystem.com/tools for detailed information.)

Do What You Say You Will Do

Keeping promises is a system in itself, a system with the end purpose of maintaining solid relationships.

Don't distinguish between large promises and small promises. Keep them all. Keep them to everybody you make them to, including yourself.

Keeping promises will set you apart from the crowd. Think about it. In your experience, how many times have people failed to do what they said they would do, especially relating to the classic assurances "I'll call you next week" and "I'll take care of that right away!"

What if you become 100 percent reliable among your friends, family, and work associates? What if you keep the promises you make, rather than leaning on them as manipulations intended to change the topic or exit the dialogue? What if people don't have to prod you into action? What if you do what you say you will do, exactly as promised and on time? The short answer is that the people in your life will hold you in high esteem, as someone of high integrity, someone to be counted on. *They will want you to be part of their lives.*

COMMUNICATION MECHANICS

Discussing communication mechanics could be a monstrous proposition, so let's boil things down. This is basic stuff. Each point is applicable to your business life *and* your personal life.

- If there is a problem with someone, have a meeting immediately. Talk things out one-on-one. If silence ensues, do something to promote dialogue. But be careful. If emotions are running high, put point-of-sale aside and wait for things to calm down.

- Be accessible. Give people an opportunity to leave a message if you are not available. Can the people who are important to you reach you readily, or are there mechanical, bureaucratic, and/or psychological barriers?

- Promote fluid discourse by making communication tools available to your staff—cell phones, digital recorders, voice mail, e-mail—and by providing various meeting opportunities for one-on-one, in-person dialogue. Scheduled group meetings are prime tools that provide everyone with a forum for communicating. Keep meetings brief.

- Can your staff, clients, and potential clients find out more about you through a website, a brochure, or some other medium, or are you a mystery? Do you talk about your world to the people around you, or do you keep to yourself? Mysterious people typically don't do well in business or friendship.

- Yes, it's important to keep lines of communication open, but are you going back and forth with a person who consistently works against you? This could be in a personal relationship or with an employee or client. If the other party's intentions are too often contrarian or malevolent, it's irrational to continue to communicate. End the relationship. You are not in the business of being coerced. Do you have a close family member who is on the attack or is a crazy-maker? If so, I sympathize. That's a tough one.

- Be concise. Get to the point. Unless you are at a barbecue on a Saturday afternoon, do yourself and those around you a favor by getting on with things.

- Be cordial and friendly, but don't overdo it.

- Never bash others behind their backs. It's low-class, and any employee, client, or relative who has any degree of personal sophistication will consciously or subconsciously devalue you.

- Talk up to people if that is the context. Your client, who is paying you, wants the bottom line—your personal friendship or clever witticisms are not part of his or her expectations. Likewise, with your boss, while you take direction and provide information, be cordial, but not too cordial.

- Speak authoritatively and clearly to the people you manage. What they want from you is concise direction, respect, and paychecks that arrive on time.

- Your children? You aren't pals on equal footing with your kids. You are the parent. Act like one. It's what they expect and it's what works.

OTHER ASPECTS OF GREAT COMMUNICATION

The typical work environment offers lots of room for improvement. See if any of the following suggestions stimulate ideas for your own situation.

In perfecting the primary communication system for staff, at Centratel we didn't limit ourselves to subsystem devices, methods, and policies. Our physical office is part of our communications strategy.

Burning up time looking for each other is utterly wasteful so we provide a subsystem to prevent it: glass walls between offices. Each administrative office has windows on all sides so managers can always see each other. To determine the availability of another manager, all we do is raise our heads to see whether the manager we need is busy talking to another staff member, or whether he or she is on the phone. There is no need to make a call, or to get up and search.

The TAS operations department—the place where calls are processed—is in the center of the office space, with administrative offices around the edges of the room. It's a psychological reminder for all employees that the main purpose of our business is in taking messages and delivering them.

Our office is an energizing space, too. Open and bright, it promotes positive group chemistry as each of us sees the rest of the team quietly hammering away. *We're all in this together!* Form follows function, and the function is the result of our systematic approach.

Linda and I do our part of management without having to be in the office. Our in-office capabilities are applied anywhere because of the data and videoconferencing capabilities of our laptops. I've worked my Outlook task list and led staff meetings from all over the world.

Intense system management means freedom. (See appendix E for Centratel's System for Communication.)

Gone Missing

Several years ago we had our house remodeled. Immediately after, we "flipped" another house. In both cases, numerous subcontractors, both experienced and inexperienced, did the work.

Linda was the interior designer. I was the general contractor.

In this world of framers, plumbers, electricians, roofers, and concrete specialists, there is an interesting commonality among the inexperienced subcontractors: It is difficult to communicate with them. Phones go unanswered, messages are left but no return call is forthcoming, or voice mailboxes are full. The subcontractor has "gone missing."

You have to wonder how these people stay in business.

The dysfunctional communication system is a reflection of the new subcontractor's chaotic personal methodology in which he or she is so wrapped up in fire-killing and "doing the work" that insidious inefficiency remains invisible while it gobbles up the bottom line. It's a subconscious miscalculation in which unhappy customers are relegated to the list of "those things that can't be measured, and therefore have no value." These new subcontractors must make a perspective adjustment or their businesses will fail. (And, per the statistics, the huge majority of them *do* fail.)

Are there people in your life—people who you pay to do a service—who act as if they are doing you a favor by showing up? Is there a possibility you exhibit the same traits now and then?

CHAPTER 19

Prime Time

*It has been my observation that most people get
ahead during the time that others waste time.*

—Henry Ford

Prime time is about maximizing productivity during the period
when brainpower is at peak capacity. The prime time viewpoint aims at
the most fundamental of systems: our own actions. Here is the opportunity to exert tight control over the most potent primary system at your
disposal—yourself.

Prime time has two components. The first has to do with your most
effective time of day due to biological makeup. Let's call it "biological
prime time," or BPT. The other component has to do with *what* you do
with your time. This is "mechanical prime time," or MPT.

The prime time concept is mind-numbingly simple and has everything
to do with Ockham's foundational premise that the "simplest solution is
invariably the correct solution." Like all *Work the System* fundamentals, the
unadorned logic makes it easy to understand.

THE EPHEMERAL NATURE
OF BIOLOGICAL PRIME TIME

First, let's talk about BPT. We function at maximum effectiveness just a
few hours within a twenty-four-hour day. It is important to take advantage of this interesting facet of human performance. To illustrate, I am

a "morning person." Over a period of two years, six days a week, I have written 95 percent of this book between the hours of 5:00 a.m. and 11:00 a.m. I write at this time because my energy level is at a peak and I can think clearly. But that's me; your BPT could occur later in the day.

Because my BPT quality and speed are never better than during early and midmorning, I avoid squandering it on television news, exercise, or reading. I spend it only on my most important projects—the projects that lead to freedom and peace. By noon, my critical thinking ability is declining and my energy slumps. By 2:00 p.m., it's hard for me to keep my eyes open. If I miss or squander my daily six hours of BPT, that's a full day's peak creative allotment wasted.

In the early to midafternoon I tend to nonessential or less mind-intensive activities. I humbly accept my afternoon downturn because it's just a mechanical phenomenon—a sine wave low point—a decreased performance period that has nothing to do with my overall intelligence or worth. Because my car is out of gas does not mean it needs repair.

If a peak performance is required during my low-ebb period, I exercise or find some other nonchemical way to hold my peak. I get a second wind at 4:00 p.m. that lasts a few hours.

In all probability, these ebbs and flows are genetic; both my mother and my father share the same pattern.

Linda's BPT lags behind mine by about four hours. She is devastatingly effective from 9:00 a.m. to 3:00 p.m., but she's a zombie (her words) at 6:00 a.m. Her second wind comes in the evening around 8:00 p.m. and lasts three hours or so. As we go through the day, there is an overlap. It can be amusing as we simultaneously hit our individual highs and lows: For the one "bottoming out," it's an exercise in humility; for the one reaching "peak," it's a demonstration of mental incisiveness. We joke about it.

When Is Your BPT?

Analyzing the *why* of personal BPT is not important. What is vital is to know *when* it occurs.

If you are a "night person," you'll slowly wake up in the morning, cruise gently into the day, and gradually work up your head of steam. If this is you, zealously protect those midday and evening BPT hours because, unlike those whose BPT is in the early morning, you will be challenged by the world's demands and distractions. They will be in your face, making it a chore for you to concentrate. Turn the cell phone off and shut the door, or disappear in a library or coffee shop. Protect yourself.

What is your BPT? Stand outside yourself and observe your energy level over the course of a week or so. Note when you are most motivated, positive, and energized—and when you do little more than stumble around. (The downturns are the easiest to pinpoint; they can hit like a hammer.) You must be rested, relaxed, and healthy when you do this.

You'll figure it out with no problem unless you are a habitual user of mood adjusters such as coffee, alcohol, antidepressants, or other legal or illegal substances. Morning coffee, for instance, thoroughly masks the BPT energy cycle. If you are addicted and wish to stop drinking it in order to pinpoint your personal BPT—you know this already—expect some mental depression and headaches.

My experience with caffeine is that it is a sixteen-hour top-to-bottom drug. People who are mildly addicted need it in the morning to counteract the withdrawal symptoms of the previous day's indulgence, but after their morning dose, they can get through the afternoon and evening without it. Removing 90 percent of the withdrawal effects of mild addiction takes three to four weeks of total abstinence. If you are a heavy caffeine drinker—you drink it all day—my condolences. Quitting is going to be tough.

But if you can abstain for those three or four weeks, you might decide to quit permanently. Hang tough because if you can break the habit, you will be able to ride your body's natural rhythms and will find that downtimes are best addressed with more sleep, not a chemical boost.

There is another benefit to getting though the day without dependence on a state-of-mind adjuster: personal pride in facing the world "cold turkey." (In *my* life, am I completely clean? No. I enjoy a cup of coffee now and then, and during my trips to Pakistan for NGO work—a jet-lagged body slam of twelve time zones—a small dose of Valium helps me to sleep until my body adjusts.)

Managing Your BPT

BPT is when you should create your Strategic Objective, General Operating Principles, and Working Procedures. Of course, after your initial *Work the System* documentation is complete, BPT will continue to be there for whatever takes focus, whatever takes the most concentration. You will learn to cherish these golden hours.

Every day, the remaining non-BPT hours are available for taking care of less demanding activities and for recharging the biological, psychological, and social batteries. These are the hours for napping, iPods, periodicals, movies, yard work, exercise, and time with friends.

The non–prime time hours are a reward for the prime time hours that were well spent. Both periods are equally gratifying.

One-Day Chunks of Life

The *Work the System* methodology calls for breaking complexity into workable components, so it makes sense to reduce time into one-day manageable chunks. *It is easier to master one day at a time.* Plan each day carefully, pay attention to details, and watch the hours quickly pass as you work toward your goals, riding the ebb and flow of your energy cycle. At the end of the day, look back and evaluate your accomplishments. Take what you learned and apply it in your "next day" chunk.

IS THIS YOU?

For too many men and women, this is their twenty-four-hour cycle: Shortly after waking, external demands of work and family kick in. A dose of caffeine generates an artificial morning prime time no matter the natural BPT cycle. The fray begins and the schedule takes over. The mind-set is, "There aren't enough hours to do what must be done!" The day is spent killing fires, and any plans for system improvement remain amorphous and ill defined. There is so much to do and so little time to do it!

In the evening, the caffeine buzz has transmuted into nervousness, and alcohol is applied to calm things down. That night, deep sleep suffers because of the lingering effects of the day's mood adjusters. This is a serious consideration because every night a minimum quantity of deep sleep is necessary for solid mental and physical functioning the next day. As time goes on, sleep debt increases, and until it is paid back hour-for-hour, performance and mood suffer.

The next morning, the repercussions of long-term sleep deprivation, combined with alcohol and caffeine withdrawal, begin anew, and another caffeine pick-me-up is mandatory if anything is to be accomplished. It goes on and on, day after day, and . . . whew! The result is a wired, nervous, and exhausted "treadmill" human being, just another rat in the rat race.

It is understandable why many Western adults take yet another step, trying to find peace in antidepressants. Here is where things really begin to get shaky: Notwithstanding sleep deprivation, how can anyone be cutting-edge effective with caffeine, alcohol, *and* antidepressants circulating in their body?

Within this classic Western-world cycle, is there any hope for an unadulterated BPT focus each day? Not without some serious effort. So for most, the magical BPT hours remain a mystery, muddled by uncontrolled external demands, exhaustion, and mood-altering substances.

But not for you! If you don't want it to be that way, you can clean things up, discover when your BPT occurs, and then discipline yourself to use it properly. Never waste your BPT!

Universal Ups and Downs

For the population as a whole, and despite individual variations, a general surge of energy occurs during two periods of the day. The first is in the morning around 8:00 a.m. and extends maybe another five hours. The early- to late-afternoon hours are low key (which is the reason much of the world takes a nap after lunch). Around 6:00 p.m., things pick up again and a secondary surge begins, lasting several hours. At around 9:00 p.m., mental sharpness begins to decline again and it's time to get ready for bed. This universal cycle is part of human biology, and whether you are a morning person or night person, your personal sine-wave peaks and lows will intermingle with the universal pattern.

MECHANICAL PRIME TIME AND
THE REAL BUSINESS

MPT, on the other hand, is the time spent in system improvement, building primary systems such as a business or a career. It's *what* you do with your time. With some notable exceptions that I will discuss, it is not the time spent doing a job for money or producing the product or service.

Whatever you do, if you wish to create freedom and prosperity, you must spend as much time as possible in the MPT zone.

Unlike BPT, which happens automatically whether we are ready to take advantage of it or not, MPT exists only if we create it. Many people never experience MPT because they don't know what it is, or if they do, they are too busy killing fires to go there. Most just stumble into it occasionally.

Let's define MPT through the back door by discussing my rather strict definition of a "real business." This interpretation presumes there are but two positions in life: Either one is the boss or one isn't the boss. One either owns the enterprise or one works for the enterprise. The obligatory caveat: Can a person be both? Sort of. We'll get to that.

In a real business, the owner is not the one physically generating the product or service. This can be a bitter pill to swallow, but it is difficult to dispute that if you are doing the work of creating the actual product or service, you're working a job. You "own" the job, not the business. Yes, even with attendant high income and prestige, doctors, attorneys, consultants, celebrities, and professional athletes have *jobs*, not businesses. (Don't get me wrong here. A job is not a bad thing, offering some real advantages over my rigid definition of a "business." We'll get to that soon, too.)

A key indicator of a job is that one has to "show up." Not so with a business. A true business operates with cursory supervision from the owner, churning out profits as its own primary system—its own organism, self-sufficient and independent. Think, "The dollar bills keep materializing while the owner is elsewhere."

If you are a professional and have other professionals working *for* you—and without your direct input, they are accomplishing goals you have set out for them—this portion of your life is a business, and the cursory management time you spend dealing with it is MPT. In contrast, the time spent with patients or clients is production work, so that part of what you do is a job, not MPT. If you must trot out into left field at specific dates and times as a New York Yankee, or be on location as the star of a feature film, that's a job—albeit a very good job!

Here's another example of a job versus a real business: real estate sales. If the real estate professional is selling property and living on the income, that's a job. However, if a portion of those commissions is being invested in rental properties or bare lots, that part is a business. MPT is the time spent doing the legwork of acquiring property for the personal portfolio, not time spent "showing up" to sell or list property.

The Defining Question

During the work day, no matter what you are doing, look at each action you take and ask yourself if it is contributing to "making more and working less." As you analyze your actions, it's the moment-to-moment mind-set that matters most. The day you "get it," and switch your focus to the blow-by-blow mechanics of daily life, while leaving aside theory and wishful thinking, freedom and wealth will begin to materialize.

IT'S YOUR JOB *AND* YOUR BUSINESS

If you are a creative person making a living in art or performing—for example, a professional athlete, a doctor, an attorney, an artist, or a consultant—or you are the centerpiece in some endeavor or another, yes, you have a job, but you also have a business. *You* are the business and you carry it everywhere. You have a unique skill that is a blessing—you are a "creator"—but as you create, you must deal with the "showing up" challenges *and* the business requirements of managing the enterprise.

You not only must do what you do as a creator, you also must manage accounting, purchasing, accounts receivable, advertising, customer service, public relations, and so on. And if you make your living as a celebrity, there is also the extra notoriety baggage that comes along with the package. This is the reason why, in a business where the creator is doing the production *and* managing the details, life can be exhausting at the least, and nightmarish at the worst. The goal is to use the MPT mind-set to find ways to minimize the management tasks and burdens so focus can remain on creative efforts.

Mental Positioning

If you are a charter boat captain taking fishermen out on the ocean every day, while every night you must hunker down to do the books, recognize that you have a job. And if this job makes you unhappy because of lack of freedom, then only by taking the outside-and-slightly-elevated "this is a job, not a business" vantage point will you be able to devise a future in which others are piloting the boat and doing the books. This mental positioning will allow you to visualize assembling the pieces in a way that will remove you from the production, thus ending the long hours and securing the peace and prosperity you want. Constantly ask the question, "What must I do *right now* to build this job into a business?"

The Beauty of Holding a Traditional Job

Most people have jobs, and as of this writing, there is not a general revolt against the concept. In any society, it is a revered position, one that carries a certain "it's a good feeling to be part of the team" camaraderie. It is understood in democratic and socialist states alike that the people who are out there working jobs are the bedrock of the society. They keep the wheels turning.

For you, having a traditional job is ideal if any one or more of the following are of high importance:

- It is a relief to be able to leave the job at the end of the day and not have a single work-related worry on your mind.
- You abhor the idea of managing the extra degree of financial risk, uncertainty, and headaches that can come with a business.

- In your job, you are doing what you love, feel a high sense of self-esteem, and simply don't want things to change.

- You are building something of value in your job, and the future looks bright.

- The job situation is the only way you can obtain the necessary resources to do the thing you truly love (flying a jet, participating in politics, for example).

- You value the social aspect of being surrounded by peer employees.

- For the moment, you must survive as you prepare for independence down the line.

- You are making more money than you require, creating a future of freedom just from the assets you are stashing away.

- With your skill set, because of your physical location, or for whatever reason, there is no opportunity elsewhere.

- You crave the security of insurance, retirement fund, savings plan, steady paycheck, etc.

If you enjoy your job and don't want to be on your own, know that the MPT mind-set is a tremendous asset. It will provide you with a better understanding of the big picture of the organization, and with a clear vision of where the organization is headed, you can make a more potent contribution. Presuming that advancement is your goal, the MPT mind-set will energize the process.

Beware of Falling Off the Roof

Presume you are the sole proprietor of a chimney sweep company, and every day you climb up on a different roof. This makes you an integral component of the "chimney sweep business system." You're gambling with the long term because when you least expect it, you may fall off the roof and be seriously injured. As the business owner/worker, who will perform the production work when you are out of commission? Your time on the roof is not MPT. It's a job, and a dangerous job at that.

MPT is the time you spend finding someone else to climb up there on those roofs to clean chimneys; it's the time you spend thinking about how to extricate yourself from the mechanism in order to build it and make it self-sufficient.

A Self-contained Entity of Worth

Here's the great thing about owning a real business: Someday it can be sold as a packaged entity, a self-contained primary system.

The ability of a business to generate income without the owner doing the actual production work is what endows a business with value beyond everyday cash flow. If you are a critical element in the generation of the product or service, the need for your presence is going to be a problem when you want to sell what you've built. If you are a service provider and wish to retire, with just a customer list to sell as an asset and no one to perform the service, how much is *that* worth? Unquestionably, much less than you want it to be.

But if you have people doing the production work, and the organization cranks out a good monthly bottom line without physical input from you, your business will have solid, tangible worth to someone else. It will be a dollar bill machine for you while you own it—and for someone else who buys it later. The ability to churn out a black-ink bottom line without the owner's immediate contribution means the business is its own organism, separate from the owner, with tangible worth as an independent entity.

No, this doesn't mean you will create a business that won't need you. You will have to give it direction and make it efficient.

CREATING MPT

The charter boat captain or the chimney sweep can turn eighty-hour workweeks into forty-hour workweeks, and then into two-hour workweeks. Proper use of MPT gets one out of the boat—or off the roof—and turns a business/job into a real business, a stand-alone dollar-bill machine that has intrinsic value.

For those in corporate management positions, the same MPT strategy accelerates the ladder climb. At the root of MPT, the owner/manager must spend the majority of time focused on building the business into self-sufficiency and on making it grow. Executing production is a distraction from what must be done to achieve independence and/or to ascend the corporate ladder.

To maintain MPT throughout the day, ask the following questions moment-to-moment: What should I be doing *right now* in order to grow the company, or get a promotion? For the efforts required to create my product or do my job, how can I delegate or automate those efforts so they are done with maximum efficiency while taking as little of my time as possible? Again, the time spent delegating and/or automating is MPT.

STEERING THE SHIP WITH BPT AND MPT

Now, in my business, I simply steer the ship. There is a great income, and the asset base grows. My BPT is carefully allocated to the actions that are most important for long-term gain—MPT tasks—which include reviewing and suggesting system refinements, occasional brief meetings with managers to provide whatever guidance or input they need, and envisioning and planning.

My non-MPT tasks include handling payables (because overseeing expenditures is the smart thing for me to do), and updating and maintaining our website and blog (because I enjoy doing it).

Of the brief time I spend on business issues, 90 percent of it is MPT and, no, I don't answer the phones or take deposits to the bank anymore.

Here is the crux of prime time: Enormous advancement comes from spending the most alert periods of the day doing the most important system-building tasks.

When you are *not* in BPT, if you feel like it, it's okay to focus on MPT tasks—the tasks that have to do with improving and growing your business and your life. High energy or low energy, keep your work activities pointed toward primary business-building or career-advancing activities per your critical documents. In your day, stay in MPT as long as possible, but remember, you must be balanced in order to avoid burnout. Have a life outside your work.

Once you begin to see a reduction in time demands, you will be inspired to use BPT and MPT more efficiently. It's that "cycle of increasing returns."

Later, in your prime time, maybe it will be your choice to write a book or to get that easel out and paint again. You will have lots of time to do those kinds of things once the *Work the System* methodology is instituted.

In This Moment, Be Wary

Once there is some progress, there will be no going back to the old ways. You will see that *you* are in control; *you* are building something good. Never again will you be the victim of unpredictable circumstance!

Nevertheless, in *this* moment, be wary. You have not yet developed new, good habits, and you are still prone to old bad habits. If the "my world is composed of systems!" lightning bolt hasn't struck yet, all you have right now is feel-good theory. If this is the case, maybe go back and read the chapters in part one again.

Even after the aha! strikes, you will sometimes have to muscle your way through the initial documentation, especially when your energy levels are low. It takes maybe eight weeks to form a new habit, so give yourself time. But then again, positive results will probably come sooner, and then your motivation will be powered by plain common sense, the most powerful motivator there is.

A POINT-OF-SALE APPRECIATION OF LIFE

I sit here writing these words on a Wednesday in November. It's noon, and I have been on-task for eight hours, working through and then past my usual BPT, and I am still at maximum throttle. It's one of those rare and exquisite maximum-BPT days (perhaps because that is my topic today). I will work for a while more, and then plug into my iPod and rake the lawn because that is both relaxing and satisfying.

After that, Linda and I will go for a walk in the neighborhood. Then, we'll see a movie. After the movie, we'll have dinner out.

There is a Zen proverb: "Before enlightenment, chop wood, carry water. After enlightenment, chop wood, carry water." It's perfect, really, as we immerse ourselves in the simple mechanics of what needs to be done *right now*: creating, adjusting, and maintaining systems.

Chop wood, carry water.

Sometimes we say to each other, "*This* is it!" It's a simple, happy way to remind ourselves *this* is the life we've envisioned and there is no need to pine for anything more. Life is as tangible as it can be when we just acknowledge it in the moment and agree it is good. No matter where we are or what we're doing, this instant in time—this right now—*is it!* Any other time is not real; it's either memory or conjecture.

For fleeting moments in the middle of working our systems, we withdraw a bit in order to celebrate the only true reality there is—this *right now*—and we're grateful.

Taking Time Off from Work

In this instance we altogether eliminated a complex process (as always, a delightful event), and replaced it with an automatic point-of-sale system.

In the systems-revision discussed here, we went back to a premise: Paid time off (PTO) is an employee benefit designed to keep staff satisfied and happy, but most of all, to encourage them to continue to work for Centratel—and working means showing up for work!

There was a problem with our paid-by-the-hour staff's PTO arrangement. In theory, it sounded great when we first offered the benefit, but in the real-world application it was terrible.

First, it was a nightmare to calculate and administrate. Did our managers do their weekly job of tallying all eligible employee PTO hours and then submitting them? Did a TSR report his absence yesterday as PTO time, and beyond that, just how many hours are now available for him to use? Did the books accurately accumulate the new sales person's PTO after her ninety-day probation was finished?

Second, our people used PTO hours in ways we did not intend. We had designed it for employees to get away from work once or twice a year in a way we could plan and schedule around. And our intent was that it would also be available to use for occasional sick days or appointments. But for many staff members, PTO was used as soon as it was accumulated and with short notice—a few hours here, a few hours there.

Many times, it was an excuse to be absent from work under the pretense of "I don't feel good today and I think I have accumulated enough PTO to take the day off, so I am going to call in sick." It turned out that too often the hourly-paid TSR did not have enough PTO available and so did not accumulate forty hours of work for the week. For the staff member, this resulted in a smaller paycheck than expected. Furthermore, Centratel was understaffed.

Third, errors in the complex administrative system invariably led to the granting of too much paid PTO, and over the years, it had been a substantial loss to the company's bottom line. What should we do?

We dropped the old system altogether, adopting another much simpler one. Our point-of-sale principle was key in developing the new policy. We stopped the long-term accumulation of PTO. Instead, on each paycheck, we pay it as it is earned.

Based on the number of hours worked in a given pay period, our accounting system automatically determines the paycheck's PTO amount. There is no more manual record keeping and the employee knows where he or she stands at all times. There are no more errors.

Can employees take vacations? Yes, they can take time off as they wish, but they know the time off has been paid in advance and there will be no paycheck while they are gone.

Now, since employees earn their pay only when they work, absenteeism has been reduced 80 percent, manual administrative paperwork is eliminated, and there is no confusion.

An outside-and-slightly-elevated solution? Absolutely.

Can you take a bird's-eye view and see any systems of your life that are useless . . . or close enough to useless that eliminating or drastically redesigning them would be a net positive?

CHAPTER 20
The Traffic Circles of Pakistan

Confusion is a word we have invented
for an order which is not yet understood.

—Henry Miller

In Lahore, Pakistan, the traffic circle is the epicenter of the driving experience. Like traffic circles anywhere, the Pakistani version absorbs vehicles from various points and then spews them out at other points. However, these circles differentiate themselves from the more civilized circles of the West, with each Pakistani driver's unspoken proclamation being: "Enter here but beware! I do not care what you want. Your existence is an obstacle to me! May the best man win and know that that man is me!"

The driving is instinctual and primal.

The circles are beautiful, really: raw, closed, no-nonsense systems in which an observer can generalize about how third-world systems operate. My favorite circle is huge, with five concentric lanes of traffic, each with vehicles careening wildly around and around the potholed pavement.

A DEARTH OF GUIDELINES

In the Pakistani traffic circle there are two rules: Go as fast as possible and avoid colliding with other vehicles. That's it. It's every man for himself (in Pakistan, it is almost always a man behind the wheel), with the whole system being propelled by an invisible frenzy of mocking desperation. As a Westerner standing on the sidelines, I see that for each driver it is clearly a matter of life and death; each must reach his destination just a bit sooner than what is humanly possible. Within the seething circle—indeed, a living organism—there is no rule for which vehicle has the right of way, unless one considers intimidation a rule. It's amazing.

The drivers revel in the silent pact that no organizing guidelines shall interfere. It is similar to most third-world gatherings of people: Queuing into a single-file line just doesn't happen; everyone silently agrees that survival of the fittest is the single guideline for securing whatever is to be had. In the Pakistani traffic circle, no one is insulted or irritated by the hyper-assertive jostling and the line crashing. It's the nature of the game, and within the circle, you will cut me off while blowing hard on your horn—and that's okay!

The traffic rages around and around, with all participants frustrated that the general vehicle velocity isn't faster than it is. Competing for space are fragile donkey carts, huge ornately decorated trucks, tiny Chinese cars, cantankerous bicycles, and hordes of darting, weaving motor scooters. When a car or truck breaks down, the driver simply stops his vehicle without any attempt to pull over to get out of the way. He nonchalantly lies down on his back under his disabled vehicle and makes repairs. Nobody cares or pays attention to the driver, who escapes being crushed through no act of his own.

Within the circle there is no cooperation or consideration, and everyone agrees that's fine.

COOPERATE OR CHALLENGE?

Comparing the traffic circles of Pakistan to those in the West reveals a stunning contrast.

To flatten the playing field for my forthcoming theory, I am presuming all drivers everywhere share the same desire—to travel without physical damage from point A to point B in a minimum amount of time.

Here's the question: To get what one wants—in this case, traveling from one place to another as rapidly and as unscathed as possible—shall it be by group cooperation (an intricate and formal system) or shall it be by independent, single-minded challenges to one another (a rudimentary, free-for-all system)?

In Bend, Oregon, one follows many rules of the road. If not, there will be problems. For instance, the cars already within the Bend traffic circle unquestionably have the right of way. Incoming drivers rarely violate this rule, but if they do, a physical altercation could ensue, with the vehicles pulled over, the drivers making fools of themselves. The Western right-of-way rule is ironclad, and 99.9 percent of drivers follow the rule exactly. Of course, there are also other Western rules that have to do with speed and signaling, and no one would ever think of changing a tire anywhere near a traffic circle. The mind-set is on the other drivers; no one thinks of impeding traffic for any reason. One does not see this oh-so-sensitive driver persona in Pakistan.

In Pakistan, as in most third-world countries, one driver does not consider the other driver, and each charges into the fray without forethought, the opposite of the conservative driver's culture in the United States.

At the risk of being culturally judgmental, it is my contention that in getting from point A to point B, cooperation is more efficient than a competitive free-for-all.

My guess is that despite the Pakistani frenzy, more traffic flows through the staid Bend traffic circle than flows through the equal-size Lahore traffic circle. It's also my bet that there are fewer accidents in the Western traffic circle.

So again, at the risk of making a stupid, bellicose East-West judgment, it is obvious to me that if the goal is to move huge volumes of traffic from point A to point B, the cooperative social agreements of a rigid-rule traffic circle beat the frenzy of a traffic circle that has no guidelines. The West's higher-capacity traffic circle is an illustration of the importance of mutual consideration, as well as rules that participants understand and agree upon. And away from the traffic circles, in the social process, it is more productive for each participant to consider the welfare of other participants, and to follow simple rules that deal with common contingencies. For individual drivers, and for the culture as a whole, it just works better. It's a matter of mechanical efficiency.

But there is more to this than mechanics. Ignoring the efficiency aspect, which traffic circle is the most *fun*, the most satisfying? The most innovative and free form? Clearly, it's the Pakistani circle. The flair and competitiveness in Pakistani streets is a remarkable thing, with a colorful, good-natured jousting that is fascinating to watch. For a Westerner on the periphery looking in, it's a spectator sport that is in direct contrast to the uptight, boring military orderliness of the streets of the West. When I'm in Pakistan, I just stand there on the edge of the frenzy, watching those traffic circles. It makes me feel alive.

These people are not just going somewhere; they're free-form artists, creating and surviving and having a hell of a good time doing it. We Westerners could learn something from that.

FROM THIS RIGID FRAMEWORK, TAKE YOUR RISKS

The drivers in Lahore, Pakistan, and Bend, Oregon, *do* ultimately arrive at their respective destinations. Like any business or any life—with individual comportment and social expectation being major influences—strategies for making those journeys range from pedantic rule following to vainglorious self-interest. It's my guess that most Westerners find themselves somewhere in the middle but leaning toward following the rules.

The two cultures' traffic circles beautifully illustrate the extremes of how one can go about getting what one wants. But is there a middle ground? In life outside of the traffic circles, could it be that a staid, conservative foundation could be the launching pad for surges of innovation and leaps of faith?

Think about traffic circles as you make a plan for getting yourself through the day. And consider the circles as you contemplate the *Work the System* methodology in which you will create a thoughtful, planned framework—a framework that is a safe harbor for later, off-the-wall new ideas that will propel you into the life you want.

Today, slow down and begin the process of finding order and creating structure. Later, from this framework, take your risks.

CHAPTER 21

System Improvement as a Way of Life

Dogs bark, but the caravan moves on.

—ARABIAN PROVERB

HERE IS THE SYSTEM-IMPROVEMENT CONCEPT IN A NUTSHELL: *For a given primary system, in order to ensure that the desired result occurs over and over again, the task is to adjust that primary system's subsystems so the correct components are being used and they are sequenced properly.*

The *Work the System* process is about preparation. If you pay attention to the mechanical details of your world and make proper adjustments to the key systems that compose it, you can construct a life that is unencumbered with fire-killing, a life seldom dictated by urgency. Flexible, strong, and resilient, it's a life of smooth, calm days, days that have lots of room for thinking and planning, for friends and family, and for just being yourself. It's a life that deals with road bumps, not earthquakes.

Whatever your station in life, if your days are frustrating—crammed to the max—and you're not getting ahead, know that things can be fixed if you focus on system improvement: It is the crux of the *Work the System* method.

It is one thing to gain a deeper understanding of the mechanics of how this material world functions, but it is another thing to apply this understanding in every instance, to have the system-improvement methodology so ingrained that it modifies even the smallest decision of the day. For this, the systems-perspective must be part of you.

Here is a final summary of the mechanics of the system-improvement/ *Work the System* methodology.

A Summary of the
Work the System Methodology

1. It starts with your change in perspective, the aha! insight arriv-
    ing in a moment of time. Deep down, you permanently inter-
    nalize your new vision. You see each life event as the product
    of the unfolding system that engendered it, not as an isolated
    happening, a product of luck, fate, God's justice, karma, the
    stars, or the benevolence or wrath of someone else. When the
    insight arrives, your next mechanical moves are obvious.

2. You establish your goals and strategy through the creation
    of the Strategic Objective and General Operating Principles.
    You do this for permanence, so there is continuity in your
    thoughts and efforts.

3. You examine the mechanics of the subsystems that make up
    your business, job, health, and relationships. With the systems
    isolated, you analyze their components one by one, looking
    for opportunities for improvement.

4. You make the system improvements, moving each subsystem
    to peak efficiency. If you are in a business or job environment,
    for permanence you create documented Working Procedures
    to describe the protocols. Following the protocols exactly, but
    open to making further incremental adjustments when nec-
    essary, you and your people repeat the system-improvement
    process in all recurring situations. In the end, scores, if not
    hundreds, of perfected Working Procedures will emerge.

5. A more positive attitude toward life comes naturally because
    you have developed faith in the reliability of the systems that
    are at work everywhere. You are powerful and serene because
    you have successfully harnessed your systems, directing them
    to do what you want them to do. With subsystems isolated,
    perfected, and then combined together again, you preside
    over stunningly efficient primary systems—your business,
    job, relationships . . . *you*. At the gut level, without putting
    your head in the sand regarding the many things that are not

perfect in this world, you grasp the great truth that 99.9 percent of everything works just fine.

SINGLES AND DOUBLES

Forget about making mighty home-run swings that will win the game. The numbers are more than a little against you, and your big swings will be a distraction. Instead, hunker down, preserve what you have, and go for the surefire, incremental system-improvement advances: the singles and doubles. Go slowly at first. Be patient. Pay attention to the small yet permanent improvements that will add up to something big down the line. It's the little things that add up.

Always have a positive regard for those around you and do what you say you will do. Demonstrate quality and do it consistently. Keep your goals in mind and relentlessly work toward them through thick and thin. Don't try to fool yourself or others around you. Start and finish things on time. Don't complain. Your life will get better sooner than you think. Your job is to lead the caravan. Leave the barking dogs behind.

Focus on the mechanical systems that produce the results, not the other way around, and never doubt that a superb collection of subsystems will produce a superb primary system.

The reality is that most people look for results without considering the mechanisms that produce those results. They don't understand the system-improvement concept. In thinking locally, this gives you a great advantage. Thinking globally, you know there are a whole lot of people out there not getting what they want.

Remember, *you* are a system of systems and your body and mind are the most important primary systems of your life. Fortunately, they are the ones you can control best. Improve your personal systems at every opportunity; maintain them always.

In everything you do, perform the basics well, focusing hard on the pragmatic details. Keep things simple but be cautious of shortcuts. With finesse, take life as it comes.

The largest problem with swinging for the home run is that all those hammer-swings will cause you to strike out too often. And those strikeouts, added together, will make life a struggle, or take you down altogether.

Instead, swing steady, one swing at a time. Relax, keep your eye on the ball, and make contact. Your steady and controlled swing, combined with the right pitch, will send the ball over the fence when you can least foresee it, and more often than you could predict.

See that each swing is a closed entity unto itself; each has the singular goal of making contact with the ball. When you miss the ball, and of course you sometimes will, calmly accept it as a natural outcome in the numbers game of life and then, undistracted, give 100 percent focus to the next swing.

One last time, I remind you that the mandatory adjustment is in your moment-to-moment perception of things. All your actions stem from this new, on-the-ground vision: Your world is composed of mechanical systems that function flawlessly 99.9 percent of the time. All you need to do is see this and then climb on board!

Every day has its flavor, its tone. Learn to work with your individual days and to savor them as they slide by.

Understand that most people wake up in the morning with only a vague sense of their ultimate, primary goals. Events quickly peel back the layers of control and the day becomes a Whac-A-Mole epic that dictates stumbling reaction to bad results while disallowing efforts at system improvement.

In contrast, you *carve* through the hours, directing subsystems with confidence and precision, constructing the primary systems you desire.

By filling your days with accomplishment, the negatives that previously dragged you down will no longer factor into who you are and what you do. They will just annoy you occasionally.

Will you become blind to the dysfunction around you? Not a chance. In fact, you'll be in a position to do something about dysfunction as it comes within your ever-increasing circle of influence.

The *Work the System* mind-set is focused, deliberate, and organized. It's about action, not reaction.

A VISION TO CULTIVATE

Most of us have at least one process in which we excel. For you, what is it, and why are you good at it? It's probable that when you are in the midst of performing this process, you experience a delicious taste of precision and confidence. What you do well is your passion, and you take every opportunity to do it. It's a positive addiction.

There are a couple of things I do well. One of them is system structuring—the *Work the System* method. I am ardent about it, and I wonder, for this thing I do well, do I love doing it because I am good at it, or am I good at it because I love doing it? The black-or-white answer is elusive but a third possibility intrigues me: Do the two go together without distinction?

Again, what do you do well? What makes you passionate? Leaving aside the chicken-or-the-egg question, and while continuing to hone your particular passion, now extend that fire to the perfection of the mechanical workings of the other facets of your existence. Get visceral about it. Wallow in it. Enjoy the flow of it.

Be outside the events of your day and treat those events as elements of an overall game, a game that your proper management will make perfect. That game, of course, is your life.

Few people understand the magnificence of the systems around them—but now you do. From this point forward you will reject escapism as you appreciate the here and now for the miracle it is. You will find control and freedom because you understand the mechanisms that determine the events of your life.

You will never go back.

APPENDIX A
Ockham's Razor and the TSR

Note to the reader: I originally wrote this article in 2002 for a telephone answering service trade journal. It was directed to answering service owners, but the message is simple and is applicable to any business with employees. I have updated it slightly for this book.

Ockham's razor is a principle attributed to the fourteenth-century English philosopher William of Ockham. It states that "entities should not be multiplied beyond necessity, or that one should choose the simplest explanation, the one requiring the fewest assumptions and principles."

OCKHAM'S LAW AND THE LONG-TERM EMPLOYEE

Exactly *what* is the problem?

What attributes do telephone answering service (TAS) owners seek in their telephone service representatives (TSRs)? The short list includes cheerful and constructive attitudes, high-quality performance, and long-term employment.

Employee performance and turnover are *the* major topics in our trade meeting get-togethers, both in general sessions and in one-on-one discussions. In our industry, it's a fact that most TSRs don't stick around for the long term, and for those who do, there are sometimes "negative comportment" problems.

Why is there such tumult within answering service operations departments? Why are owners and managers constantly trading tips and secrets in an attempt to stem the tide of incessant staff turnover, and why do these owners and managers berate themselves, their employees, and the telecom industry in general?

The problem is not due to unqualified job applicants or a general lack of work ethic. Instead, it's the owner/manager's failure to address the real-life requirements of staff, proffering, instead, gimmicky and manipulative incentives and/or punishments.

I once knew an answering service manager who claimed that staff turnover was *not* his greatest problem (although it was his number two problem). He argued that the greatest challenge was the state government's mandated increases in the minimum wage. He complained, "It keeps going up!"

There was another owner who had a well-thought-out, documented employee punishment procedure for nonperformance and "bad attitude." (The floggings will continue until morale improves!) And here's a comment I overheard from a TAS operations manager: "We can't do drug testing. I would have to fire everyone and then there would be no one to answer the phones!"

None of those three people is in the industry anymore—and all three of the businesses they operated are defunct.

Let's start with the topic of wages. What about TSR compensation? Here's the ubiquitous industry rationale for offering meager pay: "You just don't understand. This is a competitive, cutthroat, low-income industry and we *can't* pay a better wage. A telephone answering service sells a commodity, and although quality is important, in the end, success is more a function of low price. If we raise our service rates, we'll lose our customers."

Of course, client service rates are a factor, but what if we could pay our TSRs more while making their work environment more stable and logical? If this produced a long-term staff that provided better service quality, could we charge clients more?

So why is there so much staff turnover? What are the root no-frills, no cover-up, no-Band-Aid *causes* of the problem? The causes *are* simple and, in their simplicity, they expose unsuccessful attempts to cultivate stability for what they are—smoke screens that offer initial intrigue but have nothing to do with a TSR's fundamental needs.

I will interject a simple yet vital concept here. Long ago, when I had just started in the business, the owner of a large and successful TAS in Portland, Oregon, told me: "Your TSRs *want* to do a good job. It is *your* job to make that easy for them. Don't ever second-guess their motivation. *They want to do a good job!*"

If an owner or manager begins with the premise "all employees are lazy" or "there is no work ethic anymore" or "I can't pay enough to find and hold quality people," where will that lead?

If these are your fundamental beliefs, you must change them. If you don't, you are doomed.

Here are the three primary reasons why most answering services can't keep people long term. They are disarming in their simplicity: First, employees aren't getting what they want in terms of pay and benefits. Big surprise. Second, they don't know what ownership expects of them. They have to be mind readers in order to stay out of trouble. Third, with knee-jerk irregularity, owners manipulate TSRs in subtle and not-so-subtle ways, while seldom acknowledging their good work.

In other words, the money is not good, requirements for performance are mysterious, and childish reward and punishment schemes erupt sporadically while good work goes unnoticed.

A PHILOSOPHY AND A SYSTEM OF EMPLOYMENT

Develop a philosophy of employment that will address the true needs of your employees. If you worked for someone, would you want it any other way? Could anything be more simple?

Remember this: There are no superhuman people out there, but there are plenty of great people who are looking for solid opportunities.

You need stable employees; ones who are reliable, honest, and hardworking. There are lots of people out there like that, and if you do things right, they will find their way to you, be committed, perform superbly, and stay long term. All you must do is satisfy people's reasonable needs and not ask them to be mind readers. Tell them exactly what you want them to do, and treat them like the adults they are. If you do this, you will have an extraordinary employment system; one that acknowledges your TSRs' worth as it fulfills their personal requirements.

Be crystal clear about the employer-employee arrangement without being afraid to throw in a challenge that says "this is the deal" between the employer and the employee. At Centratel, the deal we offer TSRs is simple: "We will pay you very well if you give us 100 percent."

You must put your extraordinary employment system down on paper so your people know what it is. It will take time to do this, but so what? You are already breaking your back dealing with chronic staff turnover. Isn't *that* hard work? Doesn't *that* take time? Just channel the same time and energy and money in this different direction. Swallow the pill: Sensible documentation is a prerequisite for long-term staff stability; if you create it, stability is what you will have.

WHAT TO LEAVE OUT

Incentive plans that don't address the fundamental needs of employees will fail. These programs are worse than a waste of time and money. They crush morale. And what about punishment? Don't even think about it.

Before discussing what to include in your new employment vision, it is important to consider what *not* to include. By dropping ineffective actions, you will promote simplicity as you gain time and energy.

Here are some "motivators" I've heard about in other answering services: useless gifts (as exemplified by a huge bag of plastic Mickey Mouse ears brought back to TSRs after the owner visited Disney World); complicated formulas to award cash bonuses for perfect attendance; "fun" games and rewards for those who attend staff meetings. I've heard of gift certificates for having a "good attitude," and movie theater tickets as prizes for making it through initial training or for "good behavior." Also useless: long, drawn-out conversations with problem employees in which management attempts to reason with them, as in, perhaps, convincing them to show up for work on time.

What do all of these strategies have in common?

First, they have nothing to do with the real, long-term needs of people. Arriving inconsistently, they are of low intrinsic value. They are ineffective Band-Aids.

Second, TSRs perceive motivational gimmicks and heart-to-heart chats for what they are: manipulative and childish, management's thinly veiled efforts to maneuver them into being good little girls and boys. This is insulting in a low-key way. This is carrot-on-a-stick, Bugs Bunny methodology, and within your staff it will breed an underlying disrespect for you because it is disrespectful of them.

GOOD PEOPLE FROM THE START

At Centratel, we have little staff turnover in our operations department. Only occasionally will a TSR call in sick or arrive late. Everyone makes it to staff meetings. These are exceptionally positive, solid, good people—and they were that way before they showed up at Centratel. Our first success is in being able to find people like this and then convince them to work for us.

Rather than attempting to cultivate the personal attitudes and work ethic we seek, we carefully pick good people and then we don't alienate them.

In addition to giving TSRs what they need for compensation and treating them like the adults they are, we work hard to give them a stability that, occasionally, is in contrast to their personal lives. It may be just a job, but Centratel is a place that is safe, calm, and predictable. This stability is rooted in our rigorous documentation: In exact detail, we have written down what we want and expect them to do.

As a sidebar: In the history of my own business, the ground-shaking paradigm shifts came at the blackest of times. It was usually "do something dramatic right this minute, or file for bankruptcy tomorrow morning." In these on-the-edge times, a huge and immediate change in philosophy and operating policy was exactly what was needed, and our present staff philosophy arrived in exactly that way.

Be thankful, I say, for the hard times we survive.

GETTING SPECIFIC

Please. No more Band-Aids.

What would William of Ockham do if he owned a telephone answering service? What follows is my best-guess list. None of these strategies is new or revolutionary, but what they have in common is that they meet the needs of both TSRs and owner/managers. Remember to presume the good intentions of each TSR.

1. You've already identified the number one item: Pay a generous wage. Money is why people come to work. Forget the convenient theory "pay isn't the most important part of a job; it's the feeling of being valued," etc. How '60s is that? Don't ask college campus psychologists and sociologists what is most important to your people. Ask your employees what is most important to them! Long ago, I submitted a written questionnaire to our TSRs asking what was most important to them regarding their positions with Centratel. The overwhelming response was that pay is what is most important—and so I was delighted to find I had "a firm grasp of the obvious." Remember that a high pay scale has benefits that are not always obvious and measurable—high-quality performance from long-term employees. Have faith this nonmeasurable benefit will more than compensate for the extra cost.

2. I'll get some argument on this one, but my bet is that Sir William would propose that there be no part-time people. All staff members should be full-timers. Part-timers won't have the same experience on the phones. They can't get the same workout with the accounts and the techniques.

How can a twenty-hour-per-week employee attain the same degree of expertise as a forty-hour-per-week employee? Also, for part-timers, the job tends to rank a too-low priority in their lives. We want career-minded, serious people who consider their jobs important enough so that what we want, and what they get, really matters to them. We don't take our business in a casual way and neither does a full-time employee.

3. No paid sick days. Why? Because paying people when they are not at work is a reward for not being at work! We provide PTO, but it is a cash payment that shows up as TSRs earn it, as a separate line item on their biweekly paychecks. TSRs can take time off—two to three weeks each year, depending on length of employment—but because PTO is paid in advance, there is no pay while they are gone.

4. Should you offer health insurance? Yes.

5. If an employee does a good job, say so publicly. If an employee does a poor job, also say so, but privately.

6. We put shift schedules out to bid and award them by seniority. Inevitably, the most senior TSRs occupy the best weekday daytime shifts, with everyone understanding this is the reward for long service. The less-tenured TSRs will also value their time with the company, seeing their accumulating work histories as assets that grow more valuable every day. The seniority method is logical and fair.

7. Put the job down on paper. This includes a clear and concise operational manual, an employee handbook, and individual job descriptions. It's a stressful occupation as it is: Do TSRs also have to be mind readers and fortune-tellers in order to survive? To the very last detail, instructions for performing the work should be recorded in black-and-white, in hard copy and in electronic files.

8. Implement "pay by performance," with an objective method of measurement. At Centratel, we have a full-time independent quality specialist who rates call quality and reviews performance weekly with each TSR. TSRs can boost their take-home pay by up to 25 percent with this plan. For the TSR, that additional 25 percent is the "fun-money and/or get-ahead money that lies beyond the necessary money."

Cultivating a long-term, loyal staff begins with a mind-set change. Stop looking for the perfect employee, inserting gimmicks, or blathering away with impotent excuses about a declining work ethic or nonsensical theories of human motivation. Instead, per Ockham's razor, "choose the simplest explanation, the one requiring the fewest assumptions," and document a plan that addresses the real needs of your people—people who want to do a good job.

APPENDIX B
Centratel's Strategic Objective

Note to Staff: The Centratel Strategic Objective is the basis for all corporate and individual decision making.

Trite mission statements that declare "We want to be the best and we want our customers to be happy" don't provide meaningful direction and do little more than make company stockholders feel good for the moment. And voluminous multiyear work plans can't account for the day-by-day changes of the telecommunications world.

Instead, the Strategic Objective gives us an overview of general strategy, describes our direction, who we are, and how we function. By following its guidelines, growth and success will take care of themselves. In the spirit of simplicity, we limit the length of the Strategic Objective to one page. We've modified it through the years, but the fundamentals have never changed.

We are the highest-quality telephone answering service in the United States.

Our fundamental strategy is to relentlessly "work" the systems of the business to perfection.

Our guiding documents are the Strategic Objective, 30 Principles, and the collection of Working Procedures.

Centratel's primary offering is 24/7/365 telephone answering service for business and professional offices throughout the United States. Peripheral services are voice mail and paging for the Central Oregon region only.

Through intense commitment to our employees, we will contribute to the success of our clients. The consequence of having loyal, smart, hardworking, long-term, and well-compensated employees is superb quality service to customers.

Our business is complex, with many human, mechanical, and computer systems in simultaneous motion. Success depends on refined communication and organizational systems, dedicated staff, documented point-of-sale procedures, first-class office space and equipment, rigorous quality control with continuous measurement, assertive innovation, intense system maintenance/system improvement, aggressive and measured marketing, and relentless attention to detail in every nook and cranny.

Competitive advantages include a near-flawless level of message processing accuracy, products designed around the unique needs of the customer, thoughtful customer service that is immediate and consistent, the latest high-tech equipment, and personal/corporate integrity. We use extraordinarily efficient communication tools and protocols. We constantly refine and improve all internal systems.

To grow, we proceed with an "if we build it, they will come" philosophy, juxtaposed with assertive marketing efforts.

Although we tightly control Centratel's operation through guiding documentation, we will modify that documentation immediately if an improvement can be made: "Our operational framework is rigid, but that framework can be modified instantly."

We segment responsibilities into specialized "expert compartments" with appropriate cross-training among departments. We have backup personnel for all management and staff positions.

Primary vertical markets include medical, veterinary, home health/hospice, funeral home, HVAC, property management, hi-tech, 24/7 on-call, front office/virtual receptionist, and utility.

APPENDIX C

Centratel's 30 Principles

1. Company decisions must conform to the Strategic Objective, 30 Principles, and Working Procedures documents.

2. We are the highest-quality answering service in the United States. We do whatever it takes to ensure the quality of service to our clients is unmatched anywhere.

3. We draw solid lines, thus providing an exact status of where things stand. Documented procedures are the main defense against gray-area problems.

4. "Get the job done." Can the employee *do* his or her job, or is there always a complication of one kind or another? This ability to "get the job done quickly and accurately without excuses or complications," is the most valuable trait an employee can possess.

5. Employees come first. We employ people who have an innate desire to perform at 100 percent. We reward them accordingly. The natural outcome is we serve our clients well.

6. We are not fire-killers. We are fire prevention specialists. We don't manage problems; we work on system improvements and system maintenance in order to prevent problems from happening in the first place.

7. Problems are gifts that inspire us to action. A problem prompts the act of creating or improving a system or procedure. We don't want setbacks, but when one occurs, we think, "thank you for this wake-up call," and take system-improvement action to prevent the setback from happening again.

8. We focus on just a few manageable services. Although we watch for new opportunities, in the end we provide "just a few services implemented in superb fashion," rather than a complex array of average-quality offerings.

9. We find the simplest solution. Ockham's Law, also called the Law of Economy, states, "Entities are not to be multiplied beyond necessity... the simplest solution is invariably the correct solution."

10. The money we save or waste is *not* Monopoly money! We are careful not to devalue the worth of a dollar just because it has to do with the business.

11. We operate the company via documented procedures and systems. "Any recurring problem can be solved with a system." We take the necessary time to create and implement systems and procedures, and in the end, it is well worth it. If there is a recurring problem, a written procedure is created in order to prevent the problem from happening again. On the other hand, we don't bog down the organization with systems and procedures that target once-in-a-while situations. Sometimes we elect to *not* create a procedure.

12. "Just *don't* do it." Eliminate the unnecessary. Many times, elimination of a system, protocol, or potential project is a very good thing. Think simplicity. Automate. Refine to the smallest amount of steps or discard altogether. Would a simple "no" save time, energy, and/or money?

13. Our documented systems, procedures, and functions are "off the street." This means anyone with normal intelligence can perform procedures unassisted. The real-world evidence of this is we can hire an individual "off the street" who has good typing skills and have him or her processing calls within three days. For this result, systems have to be efficient, simple, and thoroughly documented. (Before we implemented our systemized training protocol, it would take six weeks to train a TSR).

14. Do it NOW. All actions build on "point-of-sale" theory. We don't delay an action if it can be done immediately. Just like any major retail outlet, we "update inventories and databases at the exact time the transaction takes place." There is no paperwork floating around the office after a physical transaction. We ask, "How can we perform the task NOW without creating lingering details that we must clean up later?"

15. We glean the Centratel mind-set from Stephen Covey's books, including *The 7 Habits of Highly Successful People*, *First Things First*, and *The Eighth Habit*. As well, we consider *Good to Great* by Jim Collins; *The E-Myth Revisited* by Michael Gerber, and *Awaken the Giant Within* by Tony Robbins.

16. We pattern personal organization upon Franklin-Covey theory. We use personal organizing systems that are always at hand. We prioritize, schedule, and document. The system is always up-to-date and we use it all the time. (For Centratel, this system is Microsoft Outlook.)

17. Sequence and priority are critical. We work on the most important tasks first. We spend maximum time on "non-urgent/important" tasks via Stephen Covey's time-matrix philosophy.

18. We double-check everything before release. If a penchant for double-checking is not an innate personal habit, then it must be cultivated. Double-checking is a conscious step in every task, performed either by the individual managing the task, or someone else.

19. Our environment is spotless: clean and ordered, simple, efficient, functional. No "rat's nests," literally or figuratively

20. Employee training is structured, scheduled, and thorough. Assertive client contact is also structured, scheduled, and thorough.

21. We are deadline-obsessed. If someone in the organization says they will be finished with a task or project by a certain date and time, then he or she commits to finishing by that deadline (or, if legitimate delays intrude, advises coworkers well in advance the deadline is impossible).

22. We maintain equipment and keep it 100 percent functional at all times. If something is not working as it should, fix it now—fix it now even if it's not necessary to fix it now. It's a matter of good housekeeping and of maintaining good habits. This is just the way we do things.

23. Mastery of the English language is critical. We are aware of how we sound and what we write. We do whatever we can to improve. We are patient as a coworker corrects us.

24. We study to increase our skills. A steady diet of reading and contemplation is vital to personal development. It is a matter of self-discipline.

25. As opposed to "doing the work," the department manager's job is to create, monitor, and document systems (which consist of people, equipment, procedures, and maintenance schedules).

26. The CEO/GM oversees department heads and systems. It is the CEO/GM's job to direct, coordinate, and monitor.

27. We avoid multitasking activities. When communicating with someone else, we are 100 percent present. We give full attention to the person in

front of us (or to the task at hand). We focus on listening and understanding. Read the classic *Treating Type A Behavior and Your Heart* by Meyer Friedman. "Mindfulness" is paying complete attention to one thing at a time: Read *Full Catastrophe Living* by Jon Kabat-Zinn.

28. When in the office, we work hard on Centratel business. We keep our heads down; we focus, and in turn the company pays very well. That's "the deal." The workweek rarely exceeds forty hours.

29. *Complete* means "complete." *Almost* or *tomorrow* is not "complete." In particular, this is germane to administration staff's use of Outlook task functions.

30. We strive for a social climate that is serious and quiet yet pleasant, serene, light, and friendly. Centratel is a nice place to work.

APPENDIX D
Centratel's Procedure for Procedures

Following is our master Procedure for Procedures, which contains precise instructions for creating a Working Procedure. It is the "Mother of All Procedures," the master instructions for creating the several hundred that are necessary for our operation. This document ensures each will share the same tone and format.

Don't be discouraged by the length and complexity of it, and don't get bogged down in what it says. Of all the procedures at Centratel, it's the longest and most intricate. Simply consider its essence and then apply it to your own situation. It begins with a narration.

PROCEDURE FOR PROCEDURES

Overview to staff: We base Centratel's mechanical functioning on Working Procedures (or simply, "Procedures"). With hundreds of human and mechanical operating processes in action at any one time, keeping things organized in any other way would be impossible. Working Procedures guide everything from an emergency relay for a TAS account, to how we deposit payments in the bank, to job descriptions for staff members, to greeting customers at the door.

Strict adherence to written procedure is critical, but we counterbalance this strictness with our eagerness to make instant adjustments should the environment change or should someone come up with a better idea. Whatever your job description, if you have a suggestion for improvement, pass it on. If it's good, we'll change the written procedure and implement it now!

Strict yet easy-to-modify procedures provide a huge degree of freedom to the individual staff member because the guidelines eliminate guesswork. Answers and instructions are right there. Working procedures are the heart of Centratel's operational model: "freedom and responsibility within a structured yet flexible business system."

OVERALL GUIDELINES

- Is there a recurring problem or task? Then a Working Procedure is necessary. Or if there is already a procedure and a problem arises, we will modify the existing procedure to eliminate the problem. If there is no problem, let's streamline the procedure to make it as efficient as possible.

- In the earliest stage of creating a procedure, get feedback from those people affected. It is mandatory the creator of the procedure and the relevant department manager be advised of any changes before they are made. In fact, they must be intimately involved with the revision, and each must give final approval to changes.

- Create the procedure with an "off the street" simplicity. Be simple, concise, and thorough.

- Remember the overall goal: "freedom and responsibility within a highly developed system."

- How much information should be included?
  - *For narrative procedures:* Add as much information as possible, but do it in a way so that the information is easily found. Use alphabetical listings, logical subheadings, numbering and bullet formats, simple and concise sentence structure, etc.

  - *For charts and graph procedures:* Design it to be simple, concise, and fast to read. Often it will be necessary to leave out information in order to make it more readable. Limit the typefaces and sizes, special formats, etc.

- Per point-of-sale strategy, we will change a procedure instantly. *Improvement of a procedure by modification, addition, deletion, or outright elimination is quick and without hesitation.* We operate within a strict framework, but that framework can be quickly changed by group consent.

- Do not assume anything. Every step must be obvious and logical. Especially do not assume the user of the procedure will be knowledgeable regarding the subject or can read your mind: remember the "off the street" methodology!

- General layout: After the title, if necessary, start the procedure with a concise narrative that provides a quick overall description of the what, why, how, who, and when of the procedure. Follow this, if applicable to the particular procedure, with bulleted or numbered instructions.

- Never title a procedure "Procedure for . . ." The title must be concise yet descriptive and make sense to an "off the street" staff member. The title must be logical so the subject can be found quickly. Start the title with the subject. For example: "Sales Call Procedure," not "Procedure for Sales Calls." Then start with a brief narrative of what the procedure accomplishes.

- Critical: Test the procedure before release! Use an "off the street" subject (a staff member who is *not* involved with the procedure).

- Post all new or modified procedures on the procedures drive. In the modified procedure, date the change, and show the new information in blue type. Hard copies are immediately printed and placed in alphabetical order in either the Administrative Procedures Folder or the Operations Procedures Folder.

- Each affected staff member will review the new procedure. Upon understanding it, the staff member initials and dates the hard copy.

- The staff member directs questions and suggestions back to the person who created the procedure. (If there *is* a question, it is evidence the procedure itself should be further modified so questions will not have to be asked in the future). Before release, all new or significantly modified procedures must be OK'd by the General Manager.

- The staff member follows the new procedure exactly. HEAR THIS: IF A PROBLEM ARISES WITH A PROCEDURE, WE INSTANTLY ADJUST THE PROCEDURE. WE DO NOT circumvent IT!

SPECIFIC DESIGN

(Note: The complex design specifications that are listed here are embedded in our Easy Template Software. See workthesystem.com/easy.)

- Use template on P: drive titled "Procedures Template" and in the Template folder.
- Start with the title, in the Heading 1 style (Verdana bold size 12).
- Follow the title with the date, in the Procedure Date style (Verdana regular 10).
- For subheadings, use the Heading 2 style (Verdana bold size 10) and for further subdivision within those subheadings, use the Heading 3 style (Verdana italics size 10).
- For the body text, use the Normal style (Verdana regular size 10).
- For any bullets or numbering, use the default bullets and numbering styles.
- Procedures are addressed at the bottom of the last page in this way:
  - Select View, Headers and Footers.

- Click in Footer.
- 1st line: Choose Insert AutoText "Filename and Path."
- 2nd line: Choose Insert AutoText "Created by." Add your name. You may have to do this manually, depending on what computer you are using and how it is set up.
- 3rd line: Choose Insert AutoText "Created on." Add date and time.
- Use the Footer style.
- Use italics and bold sparingly.
- Use the 1-2-3-step format when applicable.
- Use bullets or numbers when applicable.
- If a relay is involved, use numbering and the same acronyms and methodology used in TAS relays.

Is the above procedure long and complicated? Yes and no. The "Specifics" portion is simple. The "Design" portion is necessarily long because the details are complex—it's the actual mechanical guideline for creating a procedure. But its detail is clear and concise, and therefore not at all complicated. You will note, like the 30 Principles document, it is nonlinear.

APPENDIX E

Centratel's System for Communication

At Centratel, based on our Strategic Objective and the efficiency thread that permeates the 30 Principles document, we employ the latest communications technology. It's an interesting paradox: The simple effectiveness of our internal communications hinges on highly complex technologies. (Somehow our IT manager, Dan, keeps all of it working with rarely any downtime.)

Right at the beginning of our transformation, we developed a Working Procedure for communication among ourselves and with the outside world. Because it's simple and easy, our managers communicate a lot.

Every Centratel staff member uses the same methodology. There is no confusion. This procedure has evolved with the technical and even social changes that have occurred in the last half dozen years. Here it is:

INTERNAL COMMUNICATIONS: PROCEDURE AND FUNDAMENTALS

The tools of active communications:

1. Voice Mail (VM)
2. E-mail (EM)
3. Instant Messenger (IM)
4. One-on-one via phone
5. One-on-one in person
6. Hard copy memo/procedure

What method of communication should I use?

1. Routine, not time sensitive: EM, VM
2. Time sensitive: IM, one-on-one in person or via phone
3. "Getting all my thoughts in order," detailed explanations: VM, EM
4. Personal and sensitive issues: one-on-one in person or via phone
5. Documentation is necessary: E-mail or hard copy
6. Information is complex/detailed: E-mail, hard copy, one-on-one in person or via phone
7. Procedures: Soft copy on Procedures drive and hard copy

Point-of-Sale

Point-of-Sale protocol for our internal communications means, most of all, that when someone asks a question, the response is immediate. For instance, avoid saving a voice mail message for a future response. If you must delay your reply, immediately take the time to answer the message sender to say you will get back with a detailed answer later (be sure to provide an approximate time he or she can expect your response). Understand this approach is just as applicable to e-mail: The most basic rule is to keep your inbox empty by dealing with the issue *now*, via our point-of-sale mandate.

Microsoft Outlook

The Centratel Microsoft Outlook information system is the heart of our administration's internal communications. The task list, contact list, and calendar are critical to staying organized and maximizing efficiency. Have the program open all day and use it often. Use the task list both to remind yourself of your own tasks, and of tasks delegated to others.

Instant Messenger: If you are on the job, it must be active. Be sure you configure it to turn on automatically when you log in.

E-mail: Thoroughly read messages you receive. Reread and double-check each outgoing message before you send it. Is your outgoing e-mail clear, concise, and brief? Are there grammatical errors? Does your message make sense, or are you presuming you are communicating with a mind reader, or maybe, someone who is fond of deciphering puzzles?

Giving (Delivering) a Message Via Any Medium

- Consider quantity before quality. In fact, Centratel's definition of quality communication emphasizes high quantity. But note, *the quantity aspect has more to do with frequency than with volume of content.* Generally, if there is enough communication, quality will evolve. If in doubt about whether to communicate or not, you should communicate.

- Rambling dispatches that contain more information than necessary, or messages that keep repeating the same detail, are a waste of two people's time. The voice mail medium is particularly susceptible to fatiguing, inefficient messages. But then, sometimes a voice mail message is faster and more meaningful than an e-mail message. *Sometimes a 30-second voice mail will deliver the same message as a fifteen-minute e-mail.* Whatever the communication method, remember this when sending a message: "A great message is a short message."

- Not many people think about the quality of their communications. At Centratel, since our entire purpose is to provide the very best communication services, we have to be good at it! We are "the highest-quality telephone answering service in the United States" because we unceasingly refine and improve the communication services we provide, as well as our own internal communications. We think about communications all the time. It is a primary system that we relentlessly analyze and refine.

- We have many communication tools. At any given time, is the best method being used? Before leaving a message for someone, what preparation is necessary for the message to be complete, clear, and concise? While leaving the message, is too much being said, or too little?

- An effective training process is to record and review conversations with callers and clients. For most of us, there is incongruency between how we think we sound and how we actually sound. This self-analysis can eliminate "yeahs" and "ya' knows," deepen one's voice, promote conciseness, and point out annoying flaws that otherwise go unnoticed.

References

Andersen, Uell. *Three Magic Words*. Chatsworth, Calif.: Wilshire Book Co., 1977.

Armstrong, Lance. *It's Not About the Bike: My Journey Back to Life*. New York: Penguin Group (USA) Inc., 2001.

Bakker, Robert. *Raptor Red*. New York: Bantam Dell Publishing Group, 1996.

Bauerlein, Mark. *The Dumbest Generation: How the Digital Age Stupefies Young Americans and Jeopardizes Our Future*. New York: Penguin Group (USA) Inc., 2008.

Benton, D. A. *How to Think Like a CEO: The 22 Vital Traits You Need to Be the Person at the Top*. New York: Grand Central Publishing, 1999.

Branden, Nathaniel. *The Six Pillars of Self-Esteem*. New York: Bantam Dell Publishing Group, 1995.

Branson, Richard. *Losing My Virginity: How I've Survived, Had Fun, and Made a Fortune Doing Business My Way*. New York: Crown Publishing Group, 1999.

Brooks, David. *Bobos in Paradise: The New Upper Class and How They Got There*. New York: Simon & Schuster, 2001.

———. *On Paradise Drive: How We Live Now (And Always Have) in the Future Tense*. New York: Simon & Schuster, 2005.

Bryson, Bill. *A Short History of Nearly Everything*. New York: Bantam Dell Publishing Group, 2004.

Buchanan, Mark. *Ubiquity: The Science of History . . . or Why the World Is Simpler Than We Think*. New York: Crown Publishing Group, 2001.

Burnham, Terry. *Mean Genes: From Sex to Money to Food: Taming Our Primal Instincts*. New York: The Perseus Books Group, 2000.

Carnegie, Dale. *How to Win Friends and Influence People*. New York: Simon & Schuster/Pocket Books, 1998.

Carver, Raymond. *Where I'm Calling From: Selected Stories*. New York: Alfred A. Knopf, 1989.

Cialdini, Robert. *Influence: Science and Practice*. Boston: Allyn & Bacon, 2000.

Collins, Jim. *Good to Great: Why Some Companies Make the Leap . . . and Others Don't*. New York: HarperCollins Publishers, 2001.

Covey, Stephen. *Seven Habits of Highly Effective People: Restoring the Character Ethic.* New York: Simon & Schuster/Free Press, 2004.

Csikszentmihalyi, Mihaly. *Creativity: Flow and the Psychology of Discovery and Invention.* New York: HarperCollins Publishers, 1997.

———. *Finding Flow: The Psychology of Engagement with Everyday Life.* New York: The Perseus Books Group, 1997.

Dement, William. *The Promise of Sleep: A Pioneer in Sleep Medicine Explores the Vital Connection Between Health, Happiness, and a Good Night's Sleep.* New York: Bantam Dell Publishing Group, 1987.

Dertouzos, Michael. *What Will Be: How the New World of Information Will Change Our Lives.* New York: HarperCollins Publishers, 1998.

Dyer, Wayne. *Pulling Your Own Strings: Dynamic Techniques for Dealing with Other People & Living Life as You Choose.* New York: HarperCollins Publishers, 1994.

Easterbrook, Gregg. *The Progress Paradox: How Life Gets Better While People Feel Worse.* New York: Random House Trade Paperbacks, 2004.

Florida, Richard. *The Rise of the Creative Class . . . and How It's Transforming Work, Leisure, Community, and Everyday Life.* New York: Basic Books, 2003.

Franks, Tommy. *American Soldier.* New York: HarperCollins Publishers, 2005.

Freiberg, Kevin, and Jackie Freiberg. *Nuts! Southwest Airlines' Crazy Recipe for Business and Personal Success.* New York: Random House/Broadway Books, 1998.

Friedman, Meyer. *Treating Type A Behavior and Your Heart.* New York: Alfred A. Knopf, 1984.

Friedman, Thomas. *The World Is Flat: A Brief History of the Twenty-first Century.* New York: Farrar, Straus & Giroux, 2006.

Gates, Bill. *Business at the Speed of Thought: Succeeding in the Digital Economy.* New York: Grand Central Publishing, 2000.

Gerber, Michael. *The E-Myth Revisited: Why Most Small Businesses Don't Work and What to Do About It.* New York: HarperCollins Publishers, 1995.

Gingrich, Newt. *Real Change: From the World That Fails to the World That Works.* New York: The Perseus Books Group, 2008.

Gladwell, Malcolm. *Blink: The Power of Thinking Without Thinking.* New York: Little, Brown and Company, 2005.

———. *The Tipping Point: How Little Things Can Make a Big Difference.* New York: Little, Brown and Company, 2002.

Glasser, William. *Choice Theory: A New Psychology of Personal Freedom.* New York: HarperCollins Publishers, 1999.

Goleman, Daniel. *Emotional Intelligence.* New York: Bantam Dell Publishing Group, 2005.

Gonzales, Laurence. *Deep Survival: Who Lives, Who Dies, and Why*. New York: W. W. Norton & Company Inc., 2004.

Gould, Stephen. *Dinosaur in a Haystack: Reflections in Natural History*. Newton, Kan.: Paw Prints POD, 2008.

Hallowell, Edward. *Driven to Distraction: Recognizing and Coping with Attention Deficit Disorder from Childhood Through Adulthood*. New York: Simon & Schuster/Touchstone, 1995.

Hawking, Stephen. *A Brief History of Time: From the Big Bang to Black Holes*. New York: Bantam Books, 1998 (the updated and expanded 10th anniversary edition).

Hoffer, Eric. *True Believer: Thoughts on the Nature of Mass Movements*. New York: HarperCollins Publishers, 2002.

Johnson, Haynes. *The Best of Times: America in the Clinton Years*. Orlando, Fla.: Harcourt Achieve, 2001.

Kabat-Zinn, Jon. *Full Catastrophe Living: Using the Wisdom of Your Body & Mind to Face Stress, Pain & Illness*. New York: Delacorte Press, 1990.

———. *Wherever You Go, There You Are: Mindfulness Meditation in Everyday Life*. New York: Hyperion (10th anniversary edition), 2005.

King, Stephen. *On Writing: A Memoir of the Craft*. New York: Simon & Schuster/Pocket Books, 2002.

Kiyosaki, Robert. *Rich Dad, Poor Dad: What the Rich Teach Their Kids About Money—That the Poor and Middle Class Do Not!* New York: Grand Central Publishing, 1998.

Krakauer, Jon. *Into the Wild*. New York: Random House/Anchor, 2007.

———. *Under the Banner of Heaven: A Story of Violent Faith*. New York: Alfred A. Knopf, 2004.

Kramer, Peter. *Listening to Prozac: A Psychiatrist Explores Antidepressant Drugs and the Remaking of the Self*. New York: Penguin Group (USA) Inc., 1997.

Lessem, Don. *Kings of Creation: How a New Breed of Scientists Is Revolutionizing Our Understanding of Dinosaurs*. New York: Simon & Schuster, 1992.

Levitt, Steven. *Freakonomics: A Rogue Economist Explores the Hidden Side of Everything*. New York: HarperCollins Publishers, 2006.

Luttrell, Marcus. *Lone Survivor: The Eyewitness Account of Operation Redwing and the Lost Heroes of Seal Team 10*. New York: Little, Brown and Company, 2008.

Mansfield, Harvey. *Manliness*. New Haven, Conn.: Yale University Press, 2006.

Mate, Gabor. *Scattered: How Attention Deficit Disorder Originates and What You Can Do About It*. New York: Penguin Group (USA) Inc., 1999.

McCain, John, and Mark Salter. *Faith of My Fathers: A Family Memoir*. New York: Harper, 2008.

Naisbitt, John. *Global Paradox*. New York: Avon Books, 1995.

———. *Megatrends 2000*. New York: Avon Books, 1991.

Negroponte, Nicholas. *Being Digital*. New York: Alfred A. Knopf, 1996.

Noonan, Peggy. *What I Saw at the Revolution: A Political Life in the Reagan Era*. New York: Random House Trade Paperbacks, 2003.

———. *When Character Was King: A Story of Ronald Reagan*. New York: Penguin, 2002.

Norden, Michael. *Beyond Prozac: Brain-Toxic Lifestyles, Natural Antidotes and New Generation Antidepressants*. New York: HarperCollins Publishers, 1996.

Peale, Norman Vincent. *The Power of Positive Thinking*. New York: Random House/Ballantine Books, 2007.

Peat, David. *Synchronicity: The Bridge Between Matter and Mind*. New York: Bantam Dell Publishing Group, 1987.

Peters, Tom. *Thriving on Chaos: Handbook for a Management Revolution*. New York: HarperCollins Publishers, 1989.

Pinchbeck, Daniel. *Breaking Open the Head: A Psychedelic Journey into the Heart of Contemporary Shamanism*. New York: Bantam Dell Publishing Group, 2003.

Pinker, Steven. *The Blank Slate: Is the Human Brain a Tabula Rasa?* Cambridge, Mass.: MIT Press, 2004.

Quammen, David. *Natural Acts: A Sidelong View of Science and Nature*. New York: W. W. Norton & Company, Inc. (revised and expanded edition), 2008.

———. *The Flight of the Iguana: A Sidelong View of Science and Nature*. New York: Scribner, 1998.

Rajneesh, Bhagwan Shree. *Glimpses of a Golden Childhood*. Cologne, Germany: Osho Verlag GmbH, 1985.

Ridley, Matt. *Nature via Nurture: Genes, Experience, and What Makes Us Human*. New York: HarperCollins Publishers, 2003.

Ringer, Robert. *Looking Out for #1*. New York: Fawcett, 1985.

———. *To Be or Not to Be Intimidated? That Is the Question*. New York: M. Evans & Co. Inc., 2004.

Robbins, Anthony. *Awaken the Giant Within: How to Take Immediate Control of Your Mental, Emotional, Physical, & Financial Destiny*. New York: Simon & Schuster/Free Press, 1992.

Russo, Richard. *Straight Man*. New York: Vintage, 1998.

Sagan, Carl. *The Demon-Haunted World: Science as a Candle in the Dark*. New York: Random House/Ballantine Books, 1997.

———, and Ann Druyan. *Shadows of Forgotten Ancestors: A Search for Who We Are*. New York: Random House/Ballantine Books, 1993.

Schwab, Les. *Les Schwab Pride in Performance: Keep It Going*. Bend, Ore.: Maverick Publications, 1990.

Sears, Barry. *The Zone: A Dietary Road Map*. New York: HarperCollins Publishers, 1995.

Sedaris, David. *Me Talk Pretty One Day*. New York: Little, Brown and Company, 2001.

Sheehy, Gail. *Predictable Crises of Adult Life*. New York: Bantam Dell Publishing Group, 1974.

Steyn, Mark. *America Alone: The End of the World as We Know It*. Washington, D.C.: Regnery Publishing, Inc., 2008.

Talbot, Michael. *The Holographic Universe*. New York: HarperCollins Publishers, 1991.

Tiger, Lionel. *The Decline of Males: The First Look at an Unexpected New World for Men and Women*. New York: St. Martin's Press, 2000.

Toffler, Alvin. *Future Shock*. New York: Bantam Dell Publishing Group, 1984.

Tolle, Eckhart. *The Power of Now: A Guide to Spiritual Enlightenment*. Novato, Calif.: New World Library, 2004.

Watts, Alan. *The Book: On the Taboo Against Knowing Who You Are*. New York: Alfred A. Knopf, 1989.

West, Diana. *The Death of the Grown-Up: How America's Arrested Development Is Bringing Down Western Civilization*. New York: St. Martin's Press, 2007.

Wright, Lawrence. *The Looming Tower: Al-Qaeda and the Road to 9/11*. New York: Vintage, 2007.

Wright, Robert. *The Moral Animal: Why We Are the Way We Are: The New Science of Evolutionary Psychology*. New York: Alfred A. Knopf, 1994.

Wright, William. *Born That Way: Genes, Behavior, Personality*. New York: Routledge, 1999.

Wurman, Richard. *Information Anxiety*. New York: Bantam Dell Publishing Group, 1990.

Yon, Michael. *Moment of Truth in Iraq*. Minneapolis, Minn.: Richard Vigilante Books, 2008.

York, Daniel and Phyllis, and Ted Wachtel. *Tough Love*. New York: Doubleday, 1982.

Other Offerings from
North Sister Publishing, Inc.

Work the System Easy Template Software™

This software will quickly guide the business manager through the process of creating the three vital *Work the System* documents: the Strategic Objective, the General Operating Principles, and Working Procedures. The system is simple (as you might have guessed), with a fill-in-the-blanks format. See workthesystem .com/easy for details.

Work the System Boot Camp™

Held in Bend, Oregon, the two-day small-group program goes to the heart of the process with the intention of launching your business or corporate department into an organized, efficient, self-sufficient, and profitable organism. Bend is *the* Northwest resort town, a perfect vacation destination with opportunities for golf, hiking, rock and mountain climbing, skiing, cycling, river rafting, and trout fishing. Stay for a week! Logistics permitting, Sam will join you outside. See workthesystem.com/bootcamp for details, or call us at 1-800-664-7448.

Keynote Speaking & Personal and Corporate Consulting

Sam will occasionally travel for presentations. Call us at 1-800-664-7448.

Audio

Recorded by Sam, an unabridged digital version of this book. Available July, 2009.

Kashmir Family Aid

On short notice, just after the October 8, 2005, earthquake that devastated great swaths of Azad Jammu and Kashmir (AJK) and the northwest frontier province of Pakistan, I traveled alone to Muzaffarabad, the capital city of AJK and, interestingly, the epicenter of the quake. Local Kashmiris greeted and housed me, and I did independent relief work. Not restricted to a guarded encampment, I was one of few Westerners to roam freely through the area, unattached to an official NGO or the U.S. military. I wrote articles and took photos in order to publicize the plight of the millions who were homeless.

The dazed survivors wandered the tent camps and streets, wondering what to do next. It was devastation, with eighty thousand dead—a disproportionate number of whom were children who had been trapped in schools when the quake struck. Nearly every family I met had lost one or more members that tragic day.

Since making that first visit, I created Kashmir Family Aid, a 501c3 nonprofit organization. Its narrow purpose is to provide assistance to the schoolchildren of the region. I had been to Pakistan several times on business before the earthquake, and I have returned a number of times since. Linda has traveled with me there, too. I especially love going to the wild backcountry regions. Why? To see the beautiful children who have little more than the clean, pressed school uniforms they wear but who nevertheless are hopeful, smiling, and optimistic.

I invite you to visit the website (kashmirfamily.org) and view the slide presentations and photos. You will find some of my newspaper articles there, too. Please consider helping us. A school with two hundred students and twelve teachers can be totally supported for less than U.S. $1,000 a month, but any size donation goes a long way. Thank you.

INDEX

Note: At the end of most chapters is an illustration, a short true story that reflects the *Work the System* methodology. You will find a list of these stories under the main entry, "illustrations."